FLY FISHING FUNDAMENTALS
A Visual and Practical Guide for Beginners

RAY HYMAN

FLY FISHING FUNDAMENTALS

Copyright © 2024 Ray Hyman

Cataloguing data available from Library and Archives Canada
978-0-88839-780-5 [paperback]
978-0-88839-781-2 [epub]

All rights reserved. No part of this publication may be reproduced, stored in a retrieval system or transmitted, in any form or by any means, electronic, mechanical, audio, photocopying, recording, or otherwise (except for copying permitted by Sections 107 and 108 of the U.S. Copyright Law and except for book reviews for the public press), without the prior written permission of Hancock House Publishers. Permissions and licensing contribute to the book industry by helping to support writers and publishers through the purchase of authorized editions and excerpts.

Please visit www.accesscopyright.ca.

All photographs are copyrighted and taken by the author unless otherwise stated.

Printed in Korea

COVER AND INTERIOR ARTWORK BY THE AUTHOR

We acknowledge the support of the Government of Canada through the Canada Book Fund and the Canada Council for the Arts, and of the Province of British Columbia through the British Columbia Arts Council and the Book Publishing Tax Credit.

Hancock House gratefully acknowledges the Halkomelem Speaking Peoples whose unceded, shared and asserted traditional territories our offices reside upon.

Published simultaneously in Canada and the United States by
HANCOCK HOUSE PUBLISHERS LTD.

19313 Zero Avenue, Surrey, B.C. Canada V3Z 9R9
#104-4550 Birch Bay-Lynden Rd, Blaine, WA, U.S.A. 98230-9436
(800) 938-1114 Fax (800) 983-2262
www.hancockhouse.com info@hancockhouse.com

DEDICATION

To My Bride Laura.... Me and You, Always. Thank you for letting me stand in a river and wave a stick all these years.

To my four children Kristin, Kayla, Courtney, and Zach... Thank you for the honor of being your Dad.

About this book...

One day I was cleaning up my home office and came across a bunch of notebooks I had stored in the bottom drawer of my desk. These notebooks contained notes and sketches I had made over the years while fly fishing. After going through all of my notes, sketches, and diagrams I came to the conclusion that perhaps my notes and my experience as a fly fisher, teacher, curriculum designer, and college professor who taught hundreds of adults, may help others who are trying to learn the sport. This book is the outcome of those efforts to organize and present the info I developed through years of trial, error, and success. I designed this book as a guide, instructional tool, and reference guide for newbies. As a visual learner myself, I also incorporated my skills as an amateur artist to enhance the text with supportive illustrations so no matter how your learn best (via words or pictures) there is something for everyone. I hope you enjoy this book as much as I enjoyed creating it.

The book is divided into 5 sections based on my own experience learning to fly fish:

1. The Basics: Things to Know Before You Fish
2. Insects and Imitations: Important Bugs and Imposters
3. Casting: Techniques and Tips
4. Reading the Water: Presenting Your Fly
5. Strategies: Tips and Techniques

Table of Contents

The Basics: What you should know before you start fishing 19
    Fly Fishing vs Spin Casting 21
    History of Fly Fishing 21
    A Balanced Outfit 22
    Fly Rod Facts 23
        Fly Rod Actions 25
        Fly Reels 26
        Fly Lines 27
        Fly Line Parts 28
        Fly Line Weight & Length 29
        Fly Line Maintenance 30
        Leaders 32
        Tippet 34
        Hooks 35
        Knots 36
        Arbor Knot 37
        Nail Knot 38
        Double/Triple Surgeons Knot 39
        Improved Clinch Knot 40
        Perfection Loop 41
        Wading 44
        Safely Releasing a Fish 4

Insects And Imitation: Important Bugs And Imposters 47
    The Hatch 48
    Mayflies 52
    Midges 55
    Stoneflies 57
    Caddisflies 59
    Other Food Sources 62
    Immitation Flies 63
    Choosing the Right Fly 64
    Dry and Wet Flies 67

Casting: Technique And Tips 71
    Rod Grips 72
    Line Hand & Wrist 74
    Stances 76

- The Plane 78
- Back Cast 79
- Forward Cast 80
- Loops 81
- False Casting 83
- Casting Drift 84
- Tuck/Tug Cast 85
- Roll Cast. 86
- Parachute Cast 87
- Slack, S, or Serpentine Cast. 88
- Reach Cast 89
- Side Arm Cast 90
- Wind Casting 91
- Drag 92
- Mending. 93

Reading The Water: Presenting Your Fly. 99
- Before You Fish. 100
- Trout Behavior 101
- Cone of Vision 103
- River Sections 105
- Prime Lies. 109
- The Eddy 112
- The Island. 115
- Undercut Banks 116
- Side Streams 117
- Bends 118
- Other Lies. 119
- Rise Forms 120
- Presentations. 126
- Basic Presentation 127
- Strategies **128**
- Upstream Presentation 133
- Upstream & Across Presentation .134
- Across Presentation 135
- Down & Across Presentation. 136
- Downstream Presentation 138

Strategies: Technique And Tips **141**
    High Sticking 142
    Banking 144
    Other Strategies 145
    Soft Hackle 145
    Poppers 145
    Terrestrials 145
    Wet Flies 146
    Dry Flies. 146
    Nymphs 146
    Streamers 148
    Multiple Fly. 150
Journal Notes **153**

THE BASICS
What you should know before you start fishing

THE BASICS

FLY FISHING VS SPIN CASTING

Fly fishing and spin casting are different. Spin casting relies on the weight of a lure or sinker to cast out the line. Fly fishing relies on the weight of the fly line combined with the action of your fly rod (the way your rod bends) to cast out your line and fly (which weighs close to nothing).

Your fly is intended to imitate what the fish you are catching eat (based on the river where you are fishing) similar to lures you use in spin casting. You are still trying to entice fish to bite with the type of presentation your use.

Flies are usually named after the person who invented the pattern (how the fly is tied). For example, the Clouser Minnow named after its inventor Bob Clouser).

Flies are divided into two basic categories:

1. **Dry** – Float on the surface of the water. This type of fly is made of materials that float like feathers, hackle, foam, etc. Some types of dry flies include terrestrials, poppers, hackled, parachute, and attractors.
2. **Wet** – Float or travel below the surface of the water. This type of fly uses some type of weight (a metal bead head or weight tied onto the body of the hook to help it remain below the surface of the water). Some types of wet flies include nymphs, emergers, streamers, soft hackle, and egg.

History of Fly Fishing

Fly fishing is an old sport. There is some evidence that indicates Romans used flies to catch trout as early as 200 AD. Roman Claudius Aulianus described how Macedonian fishers used a snare, tied wool and feathers to a hook, and used a rod of 6 feet to catch fish.

References to fly fishing are also found in the writings of English writers of the 15th and 16th centuries. In 1496, Dame Juliana Berners wrote "The Treatise of Fysshynge with an Angle." that was a fly fishing instruction manual of sorts. In 1653, Sir Izaak Walton's book, "The Complete Angler" was published, and soon after, fly fishing clubs emerged throughout England and Scotland. If you watch the fictional series "Outlander" (which is primarily set in Scotland), one of the characters describes fly fishing as the only way to fish.

A BALANCED OUTFIT

Your rod, reel, and line are the 3 essential components of a balanced fly fishing outfit. The term "balanced outfit" means that your rod, reel, and line are usually the same weight. For example, if you purchase a 5-weight rod, you usually purchase a 5 weight line and reel so that the entire outfit is balanced. A balanced outfit helps you cast effectively (or as effectively as possible when you are just learning to cast).

There are a few questions that are helpful to answer before you start shopping for a balanced outfit:

1. **What is your budget?**
   Rods, reels, and lines vary in price and quality so it is important to know how much you can spend before you start researching and shopping so you find the best value for your money. I would allocate the largest amount of my budget toward the purchase of my rod and then my line.

2. **What size fish do you want to catch?**
   A fly rod is manufactured to be used to catch certain weight fish (e.g., lighter weight rods are designed to handle lighter weight fish). It is important to have a general idea of the weight range of the fish you want to catch (trout, stripers, etc.) so that you purchase the right weight fly rod.

3. **What size water do you plan to fish?**
   Shorter and lighter weight rods are designed for smaller streams while longer and larger rods are manufactured for large rivers and oceans.

Remember...A balanced fly fishing outfit means that the rod, reel and line are usually the same (or very close to the same) weight.

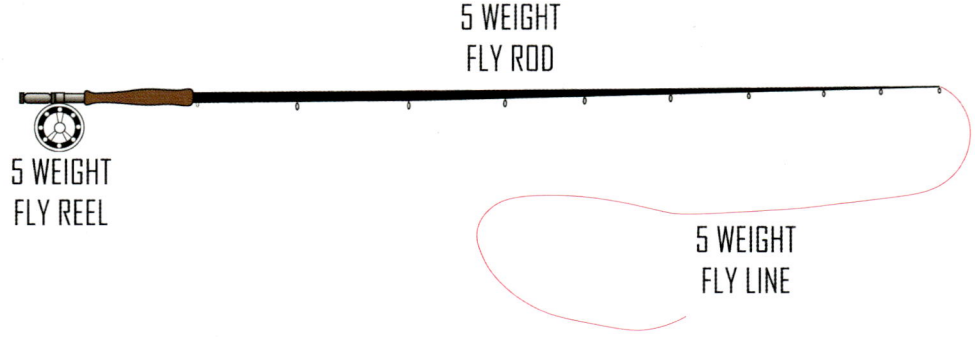

FLY ROD FACTS
THE PARTS OF A FLY FISHING ROD

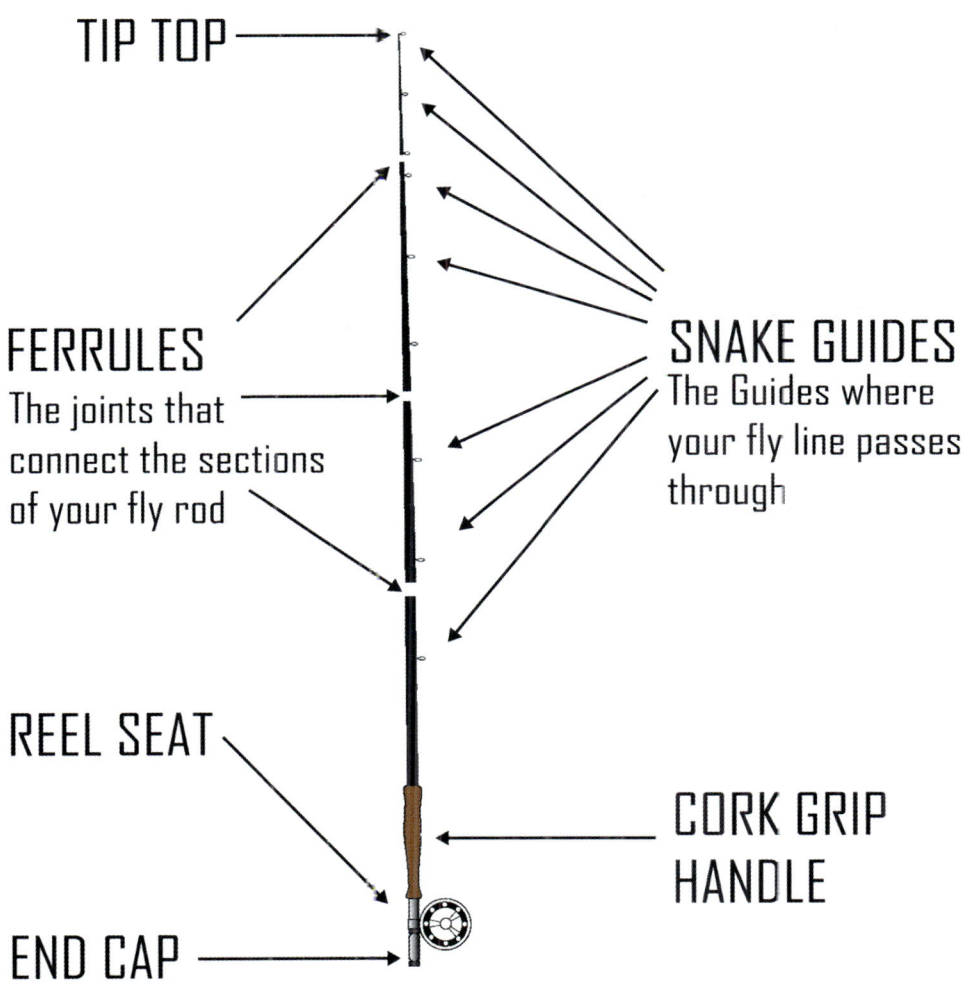

- **TIP TOP**
- **FERRULES** — The joints that connect the sections of your fly rod
- **SNAKE GUIDES** — The Guides where your fly line passes through
- **REEL SEAT**
- **CORK GRIP HANDLE**
- **END CAP**

Fly rods are made from a variety of materials that affect the rod's weight, action, and price. Most fly rods on the market today are made from 3 different types of material that include:

1. Graphite: One of the most popular types of material used today because it is lightweight, durable, and helps you to make accurate and controlled casts.
2. Fiberglass: The least expensive material used to build lower-end, beginner fly rods. Fiberglass fly rods are not as durable as graphite rods and do not cast as accurately but make a good starter rod.
3. Split Bamboo: One of the oldest type of materials used to make a fly rod. These rods are expensive because of the artisanship involved in making the rod. Bamboo rods require more care and maintenance and are not usually recommended for beginners.

Most companies' manufacturer rods in a variety of colored finishes and reel seat choices (where your fly reel connects to your fly rod). While a local fly shop may only carry a limited selection, you can quickly check on the manufacturer's website to see if there are additional color finishes available for you to choose.

Fly rods are made in a variety of weights and lengths that are designed to handle different types of fly fishing situations. The weight assigned to a rod by its manufacturer indicates the weight range of the fly line it was designed to cast most effectively.

To select the right weight and length fly rod you need to know what size fish you plan to catch and what size rivers or stream you will fish. These two factors will help determine what weight and length rod you should purchase.

FLY ROD USE BY WEIGHT/LENGTH

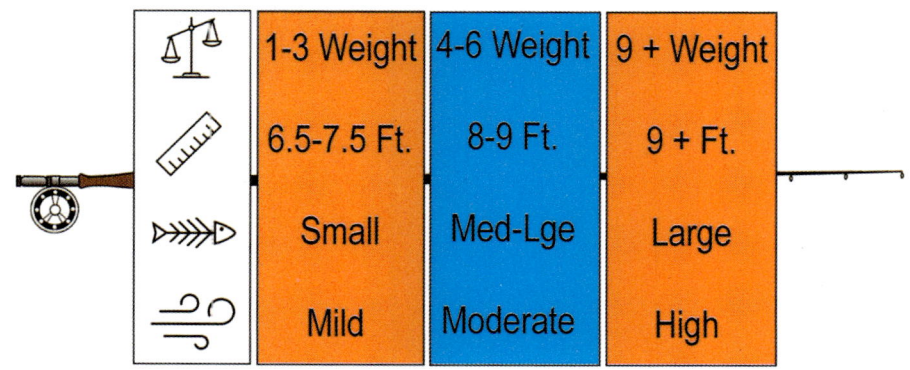

	1-3 Weight	4-6 Weight	9 + Weight
📏	6.5-7.5 Ft.	8-9 Ft.	9 + Ft.
🐟	Small	Med-Lge	Large
💨	Mild	Moderate	High

THE BASICS

FLY ROD ACTIONS

The "action" of a fly rod refers to the stiffness and bend of the rod when it is cast or fighting a fish. There are 3 basic types of rod actions:

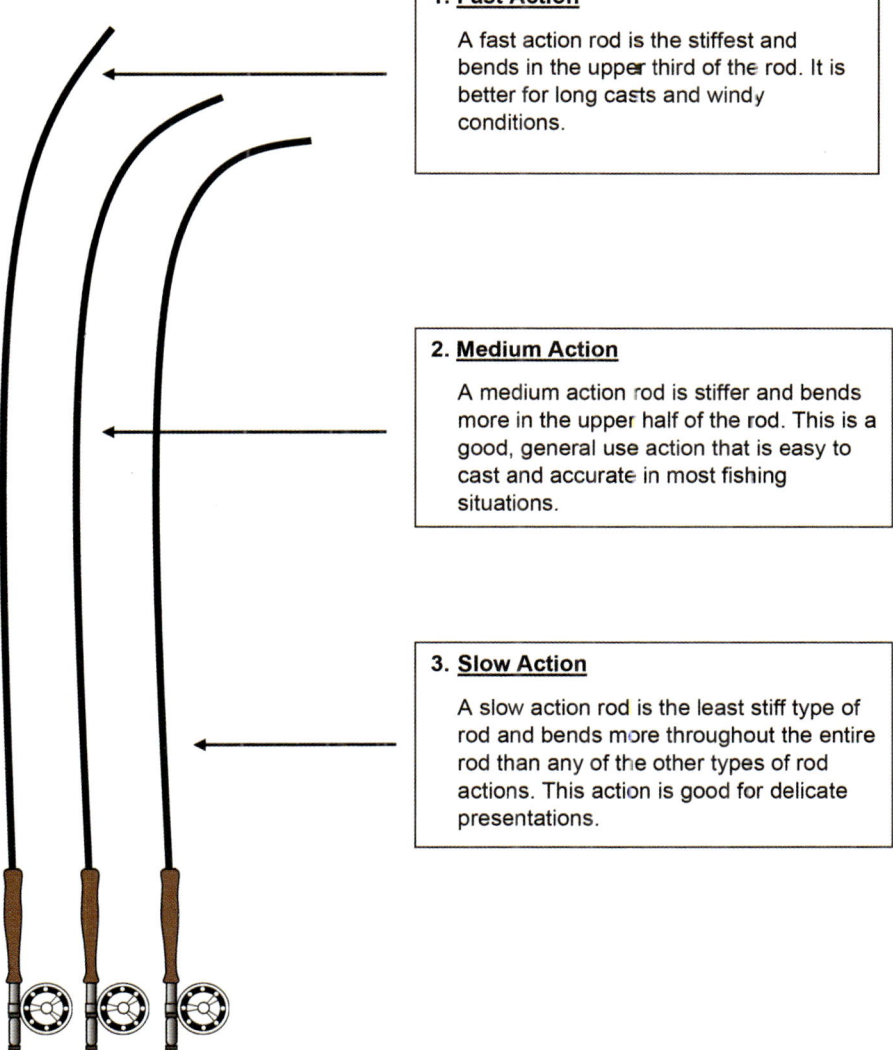

1. Fast Action

A fast action rod is the stiffest and bends in the upper third of the rod. It is better for long casts and windy conditions.

2. Medium Action

A medium action rod is stiffer and bends more in the upper half of the rod. This is a good, general use action that is easy to cast and accurate in most fishing situations.

3. Slow Action

A slow action rod is the least stiff type of rod and bends more throughout the entire rod than any of the other types of rod actions. This action is good for delicate presentations.

FLY REELS

A fly reel is basically used to store your line and to apply drag (a.k.a. resistance) to the line if needed when you are fighting a fish. Below are 3 basic elements to consider before you purchase your fly reel.

REEL WEIGHT

Your reel should match the weight of your rod and fly line. If you purchased a 5-weight rod, you would purchase a 5 weight reel and line. A reel that weighs more or less than your rod will throw off the balance of your outfit and may negatively impact the effectiveness of your cast.

REEL SPOOL

The reel spool is removable and in the center of the spool is a spindle known as the arbor. You tie backing (extra line that is used in case a fish pulls out all of your fly line) is tied to the arbor and then your fly line is tied to the backing. You usually tie 90-100 feet of backing to the arbor which takes up a good portion of your spool and helps your fly line come off the reel in larger (as opposed to smaller) coils. Some manufacturers sell extra spools for specific model reels so you can use different types of fly lines (e.g., floating, sinking, etc.) without having to change the line on your spool.

REEL ACTION

The action of a fly reel refers to the rate the line is retrieved back onto the spool. Single action reels are most popular (retrieves one turn of line for each complete turn of the spool). Reels can be purchased with double action for reeling in much larger fish that pull out more line.

REEL DRAG

A drag system is built into a reel and is an adjustable mechanical resistance placed on the line when line is being pulled off the reel by the fish. The tighter the drag, the harder it is for the fish to pull offline. Spring/click and pawl is a popular type of drag system because it does not have a lot of moving parts to malfunction. The disk drag system is also popular because it provides you with more of a mechanical advantage that can be helpful for landing larger species of fish.

THE BASICS

FLY LINES

Your fly line is the third essential component of your balanced fly fishing outfit. The weight of your fly line should match the weight of your fly rod so it is balanced and casts efficiently. For example, a 5 weight rod is designed to cast a 5 weight line. I suggest talking with someone at a fly shop who can help you select a perfectly matched line for the fly rod you have or are considering purchasing and for the type of fish you plan to catch. Many fly shops will even let you try out equipment before you purchase it.

The information printed on the outside of a fly line box contains important information about the type of line inside. The illustration below should help you understand the terms on the box.

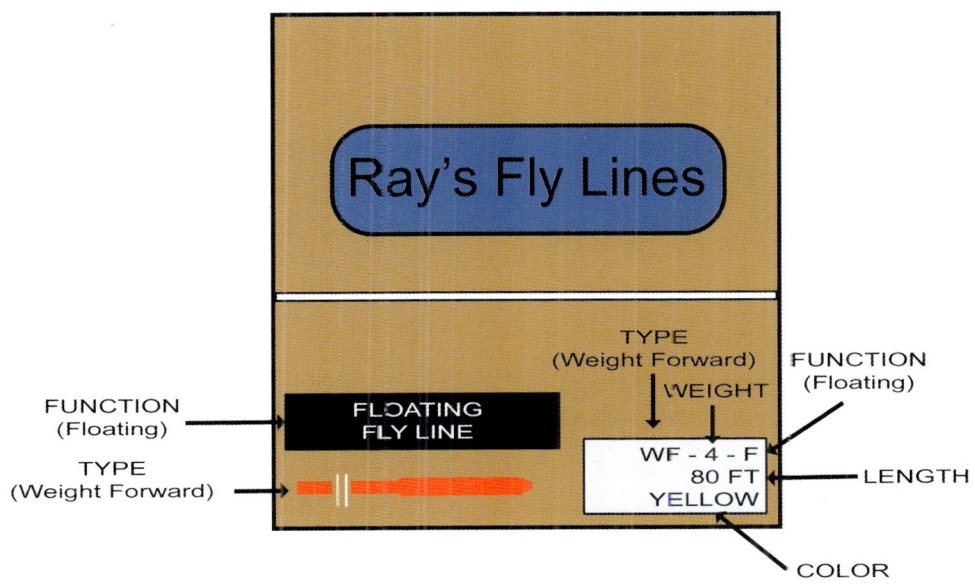

The "function" of a fly line refers to whether the fly line floats or sinks. Below are several types of fly lines:

A floating line is one of the most widely used and versatile types of fly lines. This line is made in bright colors and is easy to see floating on the surface of the water. It can be used with all types of flies in rivers and streams.

A floating line with a sink tip is a type of line where the front section of the line sinks while the rest of the line floats. It is mostly used when you want to fish deeper water and get your wet fly to sink quickly but still be able to see the direction of your line on the surface of the water. You can also purchase a separate sink tip that can be added to and removed from your floating line. You would not use this type of line with dry flies because they need to float.

A sinking line helps your fly sink below the surface the fastest. You can use this type of line with large streamers that are usually weighted.

FLY LINE PARTS

There are several parts to a fly line (see illustration below):

Running line: This is longest section of your fly line and is the same width or diameter. The running line is approximately 60 feet in length on a weight-forward floating line.

Head: The head (also known as the Taper) is the front section of the fly line where weight is added by the manufacturer. The taper determines the amount of energy that is transmitted during your cast that helps cast your line out onto the water. The head or taper is usually divided into three sections.

Rear Taper: This is the section of the taper that decreases in diameter from the belly of the taper to the running line.

Belly: This is the widest part of the taper and the entire fly line. It is the section where most of the weight of the line is located.

Front Taper: This part of the taper determines how hard or soft the line will land on the surface of the water. It decreases in diameter to the head.

THE BASICS

> **TIP** The tip is a 6 to 12-inch section of level line starting at the front of the taper. This is where your leader is attached. The tip is designed to protect the head or taper. If the part of the tip is damaged, the taper or the line's ability to be cast effectively is usually not impacted.

ANATOMY OF A WEIGHT FORWARD FLOATING FLY LINE

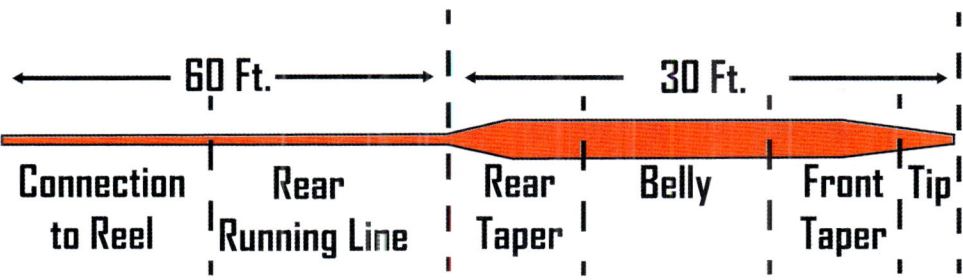

FLY LINE WEIGHT & LENGTH

Fly lines are assigned a weight by the manufacturer using an industry standard rating system. The weight of a fly line is listed on the box. The lower the number, the lighter the line (e.g., a 4 weight line is lighter than an 8 weight line). It is important to balance (match) your line weight with the weight of your rod and reel and select a line that is appropriate for the type of fish you want to catch. Most fly lines are 80 or 90 feet in length.

There are several different types of line tapers:

Weight Forward: This is one of the most popular types of lines. The weight of this line is at the front of your fly line making it an easy line to cast, even on a windy day.

Level: The entire length of a level line is the same diameter and does not have a taper. It is not used by anyone I know because it is difficult to cast and control without a taper. Level lines are sometimes sold with fly rod and reel packages to reduce the sale price because they are cheaper to make. Make sure you check the type of line you are getting if you are buying a rod, reel, and line combo package. You will want to include the cost of a replacement line with a taper into your budget if you are getting a level line or choose a different package.

Double: The double taper line was more widely used until the weight forward line became popular. The benefit of a double taper line is that it has the same identical taper at the front and rear of the line. If the front taper becomes damaged, the line can be reversed, and you can use the rear taper at the front. This type of line is easy to cast, lands quietly in the water and is good for many types of fishing situations.

Shooting: This type of tapered line is used a lot in casting competitions. It has a heavy front taper and a thin running line as designed for long casts and big water.

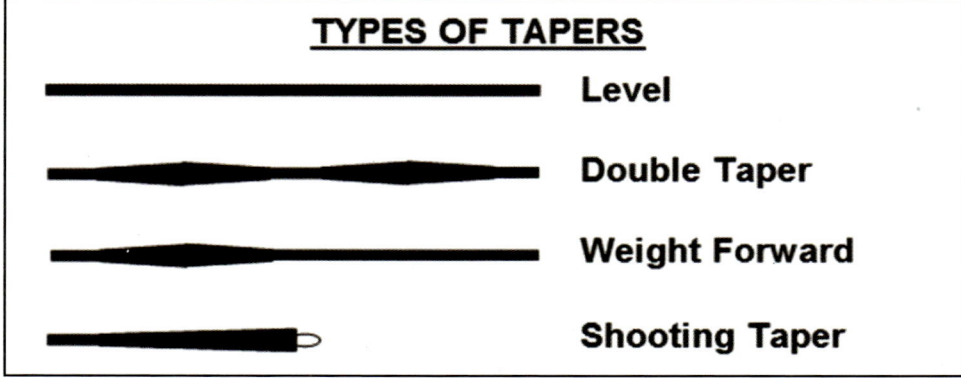

FLY LINE MAINTENANCE

FLY LINE MEMORY

Fly lines retain the shape of the spool when you strip off line to cast. The coils in your line need to be removed before you use the line to avoid tangles, maintain line control, and make the line to cast as effectively as possible. Fly lines are made to be strong and are usually difficult to break. The methods described below should not cause any damage to your line if done properly. I usually remove my line memory right before I start fishing.

ELIMINATING FLY LINE MEMORY:

1. Wet or wash your hands to remove any dirt or oil off your hands so that it won't stick to the line.
2. Strip out a few feet of fly line (4-5 feet).

THE BASICS

3. Hold a 1-2 foot section of the line in each hand and gently stretch and hold the line for a few seconds and then release. This technique should eliminate the coils in your line.
4. Repeat this process with the entire length of line you plan to use.

It is also important to inspect your fly line periodically and look for cracks, abrasions, cuts, frays, nicks, etc. on the outer coating of the line. This type of damage has the potential to let water and other debris seep inside the outer coating of the line, weakening the lines core, and potentially causing the line to break when you hook that big fish. Damaged sections of line can sometimes be removed if they are close to the ends. I suggest taking a damaged line to a fly shop and let someone who is experienced with line repair assess whether the line can be fixed or needs to be replaced. Exposure to direct heat or chemicals may also cause damage to your line. Do not leave your line locked up in your car when the weather is warm or leave it exposed to direct sunlight and heat. You should also avoid exposing your fly line to chemicals like those contained in sun block or insect repellant. Be good to your line and it will be good to you.

CLEANING AND DRESSING YOUR LINE

Floating fly lines eventually get dirty and do not float as well as when they were new so its important that you clean your line after a couple of uses. You can use a variety of products to clean and restore your line back to optimal working condition. Fill up a clean bucket or bowl with warm water (not too hot) and a few drops of mild liquid dish soap and soak your line for a few minutes. Next, grab the end and run your line through a clean, lint-free cloth to remove any debris. Fill a second bucket or bowl with clean warm water and no soap. Place your line into the water to rinse it off and dry it with a second dry, clean, lint-free cloth.

DRESSING YOUR FLY LINE

You should dress your line after it's cleaned by applying one of several fly line dressings available at any local fly shop or for sale online. This protects your line and helps it move effortlessly through the guides of your rod. These types of products cost between $8-$10 and often come with a pad. You apply the dressing to the pad and run your line through the pad. The dressing fills in any microscopic nicks in your line and coats the line. protects the core. Once you dress the line, let it dry for a few minutes before putting it back onto your reel spool.

LEADERS

LEADER SIZES

The leader is a 7-9 foot piece of transparent monofilament or fluorocarbon tied with a knot to the end of your fly line with your fly tied to the thinnest end. Leaders are generally between 7.5 – 9 feet in length with the rear part of the leader being the thickest and strongest part (referred to as the "butt") and the front of the leader being the thinnest section called the "tippet." This is the part that is tied to your fly. The illustration below shows you the three sections of a leader.

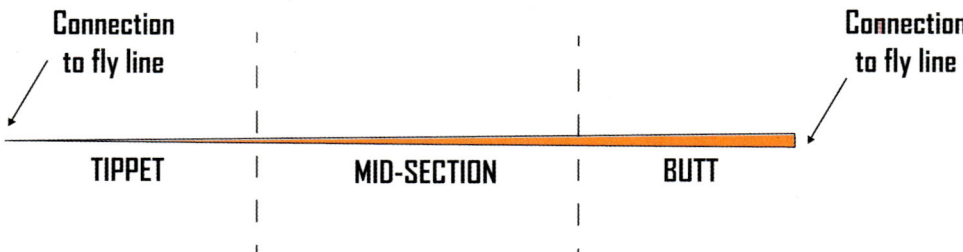

Knotless: This is the most popular type of leaders because it is made from one continuous piece of monofilament or fluorocarbon and is least likely to catch on debris floating in the water. Knotless leaders are made with or without a loop on the butt end (the part that is tied to your fly line). The loop of the leader makes it easier to connect it to the loop on your fly line (known as a loop-to-loop connection) without having to tie any knots. Not all fly lines or leaders have loops at the end so ask before you purchase a line or leader. If the leader or line you purchase does not have a loop connection, you will need to tie it to your fly line each time you replace it (refer to the section on knots).

Braided: This type of leader is made from tiny nylon filaments braided together that decrease in diameter toward the tip of the leader. It is usually used for delicate presentations of small flies.

Compound/Knotted: This type of leader is usually hand made from several different diameters (thick to thin) of monofilament line knotted together. You can remove any of the small sections of the leader to accommodate different size flies.

THE BASICS

LOOP-TO-LOOP CONNECTIONS

Leaders can be connected to your fly line with a Nail Knot or using a loop-to-loop connection if both your fly line and leader have loops (See illustration below). You can add a loop to a fly line that was not made with a loop. Cut off a 12-14 inch piece of 20-30 lb. monofilament line and use a Nail Knot to tie one end of the monofilament line to the tip of your fly line. Tie a perfection loop in the other end of the monofilament line ending with approximately 6 inch length monofilament line at tied to the tip of your fly line. You can now use the loop at the end of the monofilament line for loop-to-loop connections. The monofilament loop also protects your fly line. You can also purchase loops that can be heat-synced onto the tip of your fly line.

FACTORS TO CONSIDER WHEN SELECTING A LEADER:

What size/weight fish are you planning to catch? Heavier fish require stronger leaders so they will not break when a strike occurs or when you are trying to land the fish. Make sure to consider the strength rating assigned to the leader by the manufacturer.

How much deception you will need? Longer leaders provide more deception and are usually used in cleaner, slower water with less turbulence and distortion, where fish can see better. A longer leader gets your fly to the fish first lessening the chance that the fish will notice the splash of your line a few feet away.

Leaders for floating fly lines are usually 7.5-9 feet in length while leaders for sinking lines average 2-6 feet in length. You will want to avoid using long leaders with sinking lines or tips because you do not want your line sinking faster than your leader and fly because it may potentially frighten fish. A sinking line is heavier that a leader and will sink faster.

TIPPET

Tippet is the thinnest section of your leader that ties to your fly. You reduce the length of your tippet each time you cut off a fly. When the tippet is reduced, you will need to replace your leader with a new one or tie on an additional length of tippet. Extra tippet can be purchased in small spools in with different weight ratings.

One of the most important things to do is to match your tippet size to the size of your fly or to the rating of your leader (if you are adding extra tippet) which enables you to cast as efficiently as possible. Using too light a tippet will transfer too much energy to the tippet causing it to pile up around the fly when it is cast. Using too heavy a tippet will not transfer enough energy to the tippet and cause the fly to "slap" into the water and potentially frighten fish away. The formula below will help you match your tippet to your fly. The "X" rating table below helps you match your tippet and fly sizes correctly.

Leader Rating System
(The "X" rating refers to how much fish force the leader will handle before it breaks)

Rating	Diameter	Pound Test	Fly Size
0X	.011	12	1/0-4
1X	.10	10	2-8
2X	.09	8	6-12
3X	.08	6	8-14
4X	.07	5	12-16
5X	.06	4	14-20
6X	.05	3	16-24
7X	.04	2	18-28

Match the leader (tippet) size to the fly size so that the fly casts correctly

For example: You would use a 4X leader/tippet with a size 12-14 fly

THE BASICS

> **TIPPET SELECTION FORMULA**
>
> Size of Your Fly % 3 = Tippet Size
> For example:
> Size 12 fly % 3 = 4X Tippet

HOOKS

Hooks are assigned sizes according to a rating system determined by the gape/gap between the point and the shank. The larger the hook, the smaller the number size (a size 24 hook is smaller than a size 12 hook). The smallest hook is a size 32. The size numbers decrease from 32 by twos (32, 30, 28, etc.) all the way to a size 1 hook (which is large). After size 1, a "0" is added to the size of the hook and the numbers increase as the hook gets larger (1/0, 2/0, 3/0, etc.) up to a size 19/0 hook which is a really large game fishhook. Hooks for trout generally range from size 32 (really small) to 6. An "X" size is added to extra-long hooks (1XL, 2XL, etc.) depending on the length of the shank. Hooks are sized by even numbers up to size 2 and then both even and odd numbers are used. Hooks are also manufactured with different bends in the shanks.

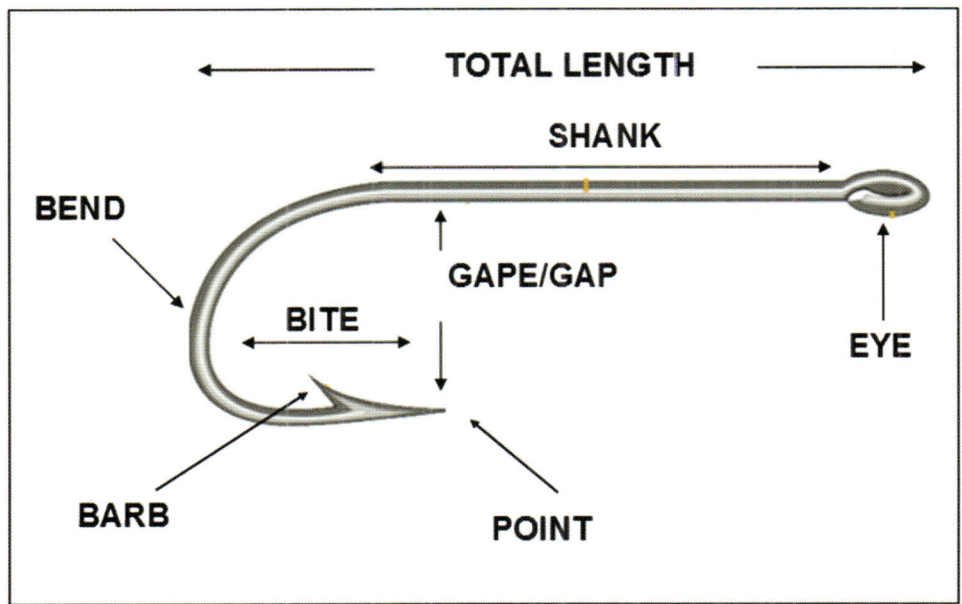

KNOTS

Below is an illustration of the knots that are typically used in fly fishing. How to tie each knot is illustrated on the next few pages. These are important knots to learn and practice tying.

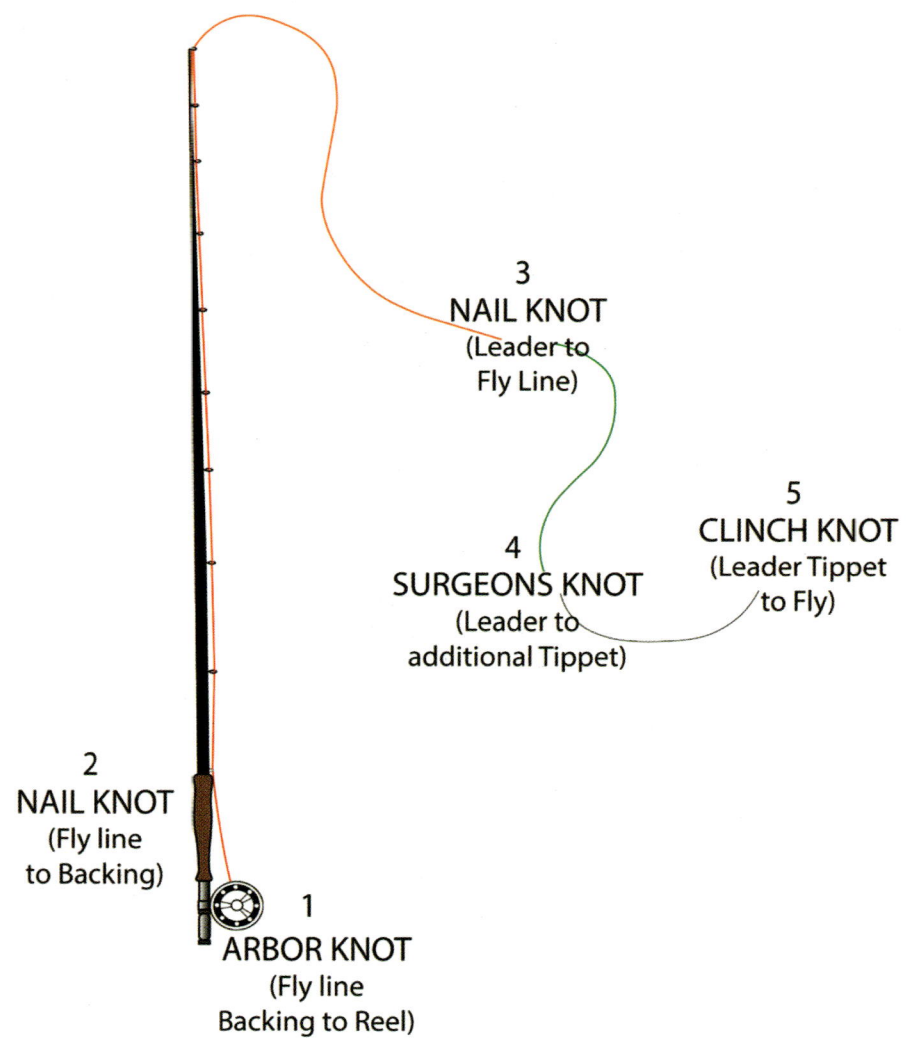

THE BASICS

ARBOR KNOT

This is an easy knot to learn to tie but one that you will not use that often. This knot is used to attach your fly line backing to the arbor on your reel spool.

STEPS:

1. Thread the line around the arbor of the spool (1 & 2).
2. Tie an overhand knot in the backing line (3 & 4).
3. Tie a second overhand knot in the tag end of the backing (5, 6, 7).
4. Grab on either side of the knots and pull to tighten
5. Trim the excess (8)

Test the knot by pulling on the section of fly line backing tied to the Arbor.

You will tie a Nail knot to connect your fly line backing to the end of your fly line (1)

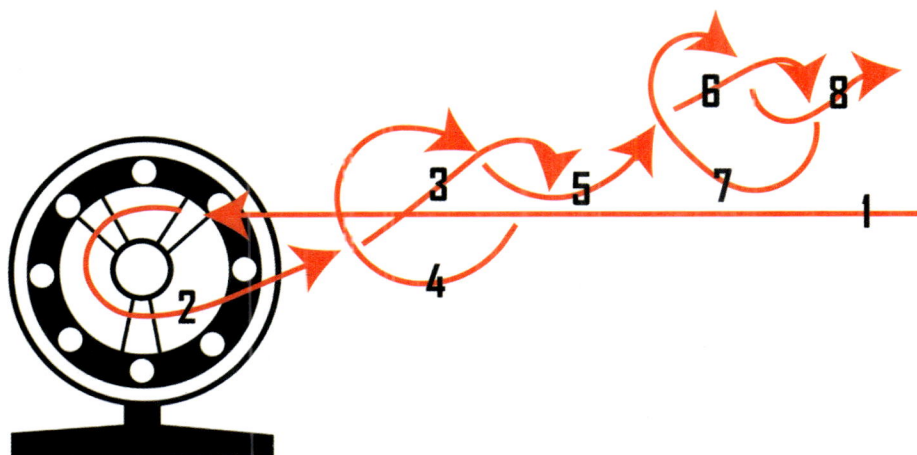

KNOTS | 37

NAIL KNOT

The Nail knot is a more difficult knot to tie. It is used to connect your backing to the end of your fly line. It requires more practice than other knots and is a knot that you will not use too often. There are Nail knot tools sold that help make tying this knot easier.

S T E P S :

1. Place a nail, small tube, or nail knot tool between the fly line and leader (1) and wrap the leader back towards the end of your fly line 5-6 times (2-7).
2. Pass the end of the leader back through the loops you just made (8) and pull on both ends (9 & 10) trying not to have the loops cross each other.
3. Remove the knot, moisten it with saliva or water and pull both ends in opposite directions to tighten and clip tags.
4. Test the knot by pulling on the fly line backing and fly line.
5. Trim the excess.

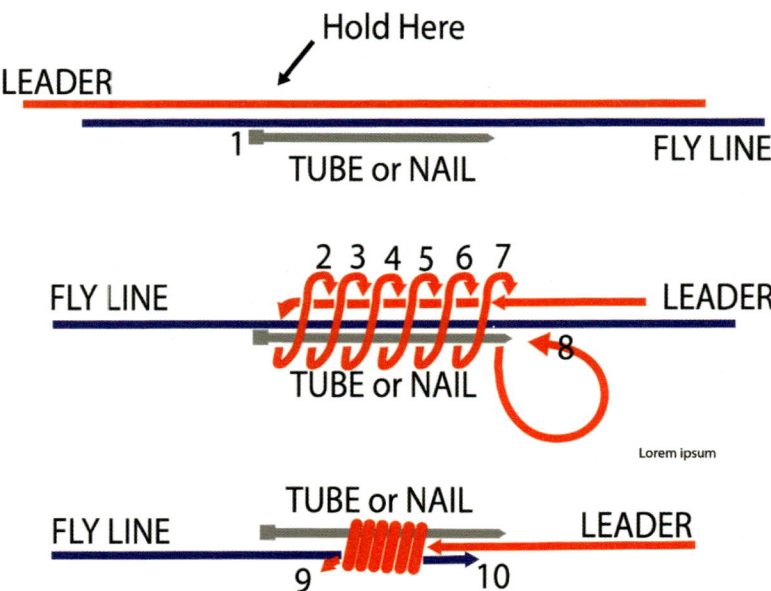

Lorem ipsum

THE BASICS

DOUBLE/TRIPLE SURGEONS KNOT

The Double/Triple Surgeons knot is used to connect extra tippet to your leader when as it is reduced when you cut off flies. This is a knot that you will use often so practice it until tying it is easy.

Remember that you are only adding enough tippet to restore your leader to its original length. Use the formula below to determine the correct size tippet to add.

STEPS:

1. Position your leader and the extra length of tippet you are adding alongside of each other and overlapping about 10 inches (1 & 2).
2. Working the two lines as one and tie an Overhand Knot (3). It will be necessary to pull one line (e.g., the leader) completely through this loop.
3. Pull the leader through this loop again (4). Pass the other end through the loop (5-7) and repeat the last step for a triple surgeon's knot.
4. Moisten the knot with saliva or water and form the knot.
5. Trim the excess.

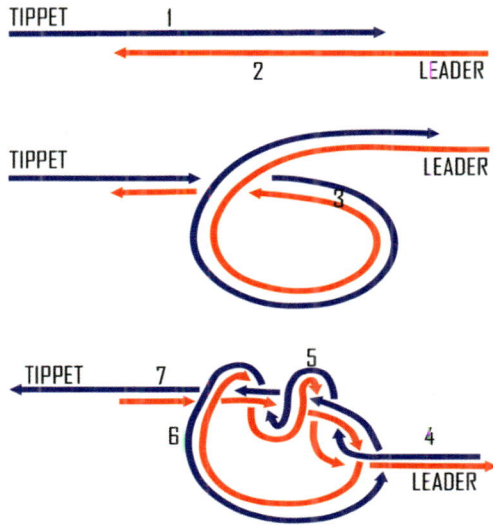

KNOTS | 39

IMPROVED CLINCH KNOT

This knot is used to attach the end of your tippet to your fly.

STEPS:

1. Thread your tippet through the eye of your fly and allow at least 3 inches beyond the eye (1 and 2).
2. Wrap the tag end of your tippet 5 - 6 times around the tippet/leader away from your fly line. (3-8)
3. Pass the tag end through the first loop above the eye of the hook, over the coils, and through the larger loop (9).
4. Moisten the knot with saliva and tighten by pulling the tag end and tippet/leader going to your line together.
5. Trim the excess.

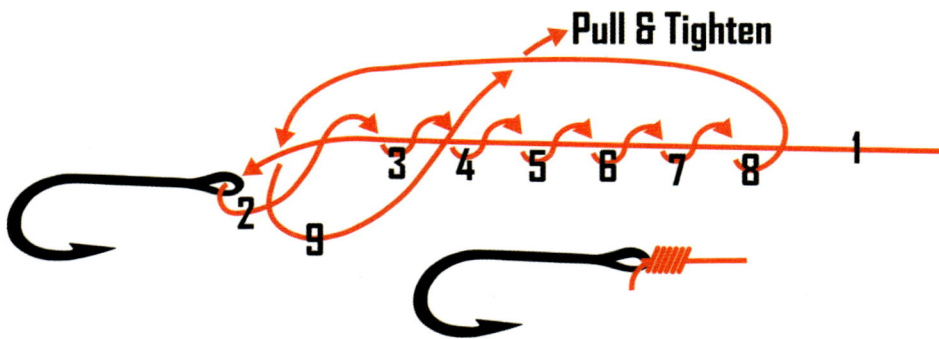

THE BASICS

PERFECTION LOOP

This is a useful knot to create a loop in a line or make a loop-to-loop connection that can be used to connect your fly line and leader if they do not have loops. Keep in mind that you can buy fly lines and leaders with loops in the ends or you can purchase loops that can be attached to the end of your fly line.

STEPS:

1. Make a loop in the line (1), bring the tail end around the back (2), and bring the tail end around the back of the first loop (3) and over the second loop.
2. Pass the tail end through the second loop (4) and then through the first loop (5).
3. Moisten the loops, draw tight and trim.
4. Trim the excess.

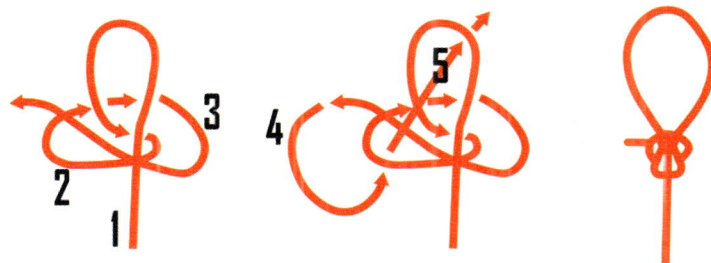

ESSENTIAL EQUIPMENT

There are a lot of fly fishing gadgets and gizmos to purchase but below is a list of the essential pieces of equipment that I would recommend purchasing when you are first starting out.

Polarized sunglasses: Important for reducing the glare and letting you see fish underwater.

Hat: Keeps the sun off your head and face and protects you from erratically cast flies.

Sun Block: Protects you from the sun overhead and rays reflected off the water.

Net: Purchase a net made of material that will not harm fish, that is large enough to hold the type of fish you catch, and not too heavy to carry all day.

Dry/Wet Fly Treatment: Specially made chemicals that apply to wet flies (to sink faster) and dry flies (to float better).

Retractor (Zinger): Thin retractable cord with a device that attaches to a piece of equipment (pliers, knife, forceps, etc.) and your vest to prevent the piece of equipment from falling into the water.

Safety Whistle: Buy a waterproof safety whistle that you can use to signal for help if you get into trouble while wading.

Pliers/Forceps: Used to remove the fly from a fish's mouth, your hat, wading jacket, etc. Also used to crush the barb's on your hooks so they cause less damage to a fish.

Knife: A small knife is useful for many purposes.

Vests and Packs: Fly fishers are like turtles, we carry everything with us. The vest or pack that you select should feel comfortable on you while you cast and maneuver around in and out of the water and have enough space to store all the gear you need. I suggest trying on a few different styles to determine which one feels comfortable. Select a vest size that is big enough to fit over the type of clothes you wear when you fish in different seasons. Packs are made to be worn on your waist, chest or back. Some vests and packs are modular and additional items can be added as needed. I own a modular backpack that also has two front chest pouches that detach and can be worn on their own.

Wading Staff: A wading staff is an important safety tool that can be used to test the depth of the water, stabilize you in the water, and keep you upright if you wade in to deeply, get stuck in the muck, or lose your footing and begin to fall over into the water. Collapsible or retractable wading staffs are lightweight and can be attached to your wading belt, so they do not float away if dropped, are available when you need them, and out of the way when you do not.

THE BASICS

Waders are waterproof pants that keep you dry while you are in the water. There are two basic types of waders:

NEOPRENE WADERS

Made of heavy rubberized material and retain body moisture. They provide the most warmth in cold water, are durable and harder to rip/tear, are hot in warm weather, and are more difficult to move in due to their weight. They usually have rubber boots attached that cannot be removed.

BREATHABLE WADERS

Made of a lighter weight waterproof fabric that does not retain body moisture. You can wear heavier clothing underneath to stay warm in colder weather. They rip or tear more easily if caught on something sharp but can be patched. The feet are made of neoprene, and you will need to buy a separate set of wading boots.

Waders are made in leg, hip and chest styles with chest waders being the most popular and flexible type. The Chest waders allow you to fish in deeper water and the top part can be rolled down in warmer weather. Maintenance of your waders is easy by simply rinsing them off with fresh water and keeping them away from sharp objects.

A wading jacket is also made of waterproof material and is useful when for additional protection while fishing when it is cold, rainy or snowy. The jacket can easily be stored in a pack and used when needed. A wading jacket is worn over your waders and can be worn over your vest if you are using one.

If you buy stocking foot waders you will also need to purchase wading boots. The boots provide stability, ankle support, and traction in the water because rocks and other debris can be slippery. Wading boots come in a variety of styles and usually come with felt or rubber soles. Some boots also have studded soles for fishing in rough terrain. Felt soles are no longer allowed by Fish and Wildlife Divisions in some states because the felt has the potential to transfer invasive species from one water source to another if you fish in different rivers and don't dry the soles of your boots. I own a pair of wading boots with interchangeable soles (felt, rubber and studded) so I can adapt to different situations.

Wear a heavy sock when you try on wading boots or ask to put on a pair of waders with neoprene feet and then try on the boots to make sure you buy the correct size of boot.

WADING

The banks of many rivers and streams are lined with obstructions (e.g., trees, bushes, etc.) that make it difficult to cast and fly fish from the land so a majority of fly fishing is done while wading in the water. Wading is an essential skill to master because it allows you to position yourself in relation to where fish are or may be holding (These spots are known as prime lies and are discussed later in this book).

Stealth is an important skill when wading. You want to avoid kicking up debris and gravel that can travel downstream and alert fish to your presence and potentially frighten them away.

Safety is a major concern when wading and one small slip will land you in the water with the potential for your waders to start filling up with water. Below are some tips to remain safe while wading:

1. Don't step forward unless you are reasonable sure you will not slip or the water is not too deep. Be cautious of wobbly or slimy rocks or logs that can move once you step on them. I try and test my steps and use my wading stick to help balance me in case I do slip or start to fall, especially if I cannot see the bottom.
2. Use polarized glasses to reduce glare and help you see obstructions beneath the surface. I attach my glasses to a lanyard, so I won't lose them in the water.
3. Plan a safety route out of the water in the event of an emergency once you arrive at a spot to fish.
4. Do not wade too deeply in the water so that you have trouble getting safely back out. Once the current starts pushing against you it can become more difficult to move out.
5. Carry a waterproof safety whistle in your vest in case you need to signal for help.
6. Use a wading staff to help with balance and for added stability in the water.
7. Wear a wading belt and keep it snug enough that it will slow down water from rushing into your waders if you did fall.
8. If you fall into the water while wearing waders and they start to fill up, try and stand back up and exit the water. If you start to drift downstream, point your legs downward and try to keep your boots out of the water, spread your arms like a flying bird, and try and paddle yourself toward shallow water.

THE BASICS

SAFELY RELEASING A FISH

Many fly fishers practice "catch and release" which means that you release the fish unharmed and alive to grow and be caught again another day. Trout are delicate and have a protective slime that coat their skin. It is important to handle them as little as possible and to wet your hand first if you have to hold the fish to release it. I use pliers to crush the barbs on my hooks because it makes it easier to remove the hook and causes less harm to the fish.

How to Properly Release a Fish

1. Net the fish and keep the fish in the water.
2. Turn the fish on its side or back which will cause it to relax and reduce its movements.
3. Grab the hook with your forceps and gently remove it by turning it side to side.
4. Try not to damage the fish's gills by putting your fingers into them or squeezing the fish too hard and damaging its internal organs.
5. Make sure that the fish is completely revived before you release it back into the water. You can keep the fish in your net in the water facing upstream (if the current isn't too strong) or move the fish back and forth in a slower current so the water moves over its gills to revive it. The fish should be able to swim away on its own. Do not toss or throw the fish back into the water.

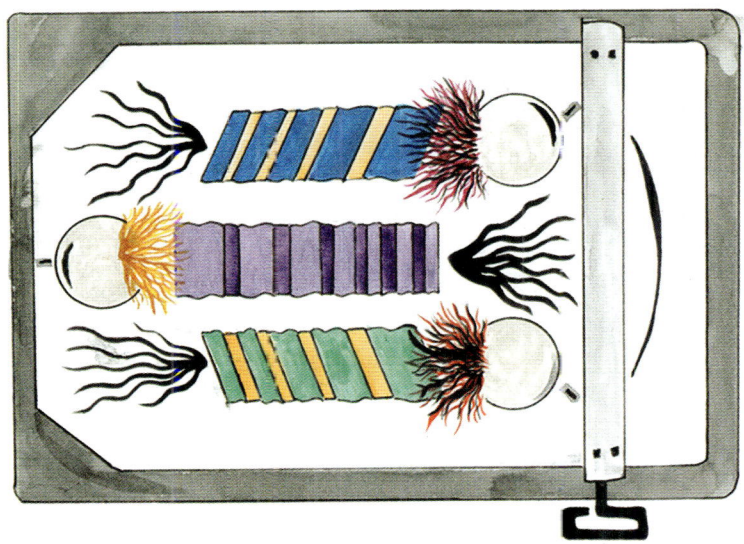

INSECTS AND IMITATION
Important Bugs and Imposters

THE HATCH

The diet of trout and other freshwater fish consists of a variety of aquatic insects, terrestrials, amphibians, crustaceans, leeches, worms, and other food available to them throughout the year. The term "hatch," refers to when an aquatic insect begins to transform from its immature stage to the adult phase of its life. The term "matching the hatch" is when you select an imitation fly that matches the type of insects or food fish are eating at the time you are fishing.

Trout feed on insects at all levels of the water column depending on what is available to them at the time. They might feed on immature insects on the bottom, as insects rise up toward the surface, when the insect floats on the surface to dry its wings, or jump out of the water to catch an insect in the air, or when the insect dies and falls onto the surface of the water.

Hatches of aquatic insects occur in relation to seasonal changes and temperature. Not all species of insects are native to all bodies of water which means that different types of insects live in rivers and streams in different regions. If you are traveling to another state to fish, make sure that you do some research and find a hatch chart for the specific body of water that you plan to fish. Online fly fishing groups can be found and are always a great source of information.

Hatch charts are one tool that can help you match the correct imitation fly to the real insects that are supposed to be hatching at a specific time of the year. Hatch charts are general guides because they can't consider real-time weather and water conditions. I suggest using the hatch chart in conjunction with real-time information from people who have fished the river (check at local fly shops) or your own observations at the river.

INSECTS AND IMITATION

BEFORE YOU FISH

Review the hatch chart for the river where you plan to fish, talk with people at a fly shop near the river or stream to find out what insects have been hatching, what flies have been successfully used to catch fish, the water conditions, etc. before you start to fish. I also recommend searching online to see if there are any websites that offer you this type of information. Many states have departments of fish and wildlife and maintain websites with this type of information.

WHILE YOU FISH

When you get to the river, look and see what fish are eating. Sometimes nothing is visible but try using a seine net (a small handheld net) to skim the water and gravel at the bottom to see what insects are present. Look on and under rocks, in bushes on the bank, and at spider webs to see what type of insects you can find. Observe the water to see how fish are rising to feed and determine what those rises tell you about what fish might be eating and at what level of the water column the fish are eating (see the information on rises later in this book).

AFTER YOU FISH

Write down some notes after you have fished. I take notes on the location I was fishing, the time of day, the temperature of the water and air, if it was raining or snowing, the types of insects I observed and their lifecycle stages, the flies I used that were/weren't successful.

Hatch charts are designed to help you identify the pattern and size of fly to use at specific times of the year to match what is supposed to be hatching. Not all hatch charts are the same and may not provide the size and color of the fly to use. I try and carry the same type of fly in a few different sizes and colors based on the hatch chart so that I am prepared for what can be hatching when I am fishing.

I also carry fly patterns that represent the different lifecycle stages of the insects that live in the water where I fish. You may get to a river an fish at feeding on insects below the surface and then the temperature gets warmer and the sun comes out and insects start to hatch and fish are now feeding on the surface. Having flies at different lifecycle stages helps you match the hatch.

Across the top of a hatch chart you usually find the months and some indication of how long the potential fly pattern should be used. Keep in mind that hatch charts cannot predict the real-time weather conditions on the river.

SAMPLE HATCH CHART

	Hook #	Apr	May	Jun	Jul	Aug	Sep	Oct	Nov	Dec
Black Caddis	12 - 22	X								
Blue Quill	18 - 20	X								
Quill Gordon	14 - 16	X	X							
Hendrickson	14	X	X							
March Brown	10 - 12		X							
Brown Drakes	8 - 10		X	X						
Cream Midges	18 - 22			X						
Associated Midges	18 - 28		X	X	X	X	X	X	X	
Sulphurs	16		X	X						
Light Cahill	14 - 16		X	X						
Blue Winged Olives	18 - 24	X	X	X	X	X	X	X	X	X
Pale Evening Dun	14 - 22		X	X	X					
Caddis	12 - 22	X	X	X	X	X	X	X		
Isoynchia	12 - 16		X	X	X	X	X	X		
Stoneflies			Black, Golden, Brown - All Year							

On the chart above you can see that a Pale Evening Dun fly pattern (size 14-22 depending on the size of the insects available to fish at that time) is suggested to be used May - July. The chart cannot consider if May is a warmer of colder month that average and delays or escalates the insect hatch. Fly shops near the place where you are fishing usually have very up-to-date info on the types of insects hatching and the flies being used to catch fish.

The table to the right shows you where specific types of insect hatches usually occur. An insect that hatches on land will usually be more unfamiliar to fish at that specific stage of its life.

INSECTS AND IMITATION

	Where the Hatch Usually Occurs		
Type	Land	Subsurface	Surface
Mayflies	X	X	X
Caddis Flies	X	X	X
Stone Flies	X		
Midges			X
Dragon and Damselflies	X		
Terrestrials	X		
Scuds		X	
Crustaceans		X	

THE HATCH

MAYFLIES

Ephemeroptera (E-FEM-ER-OP-TUR-UH - short-lived, winged)

A Mayfly matures in 5 life stages with stages 2-5 being the most important food sources for fish. The stages include: (1) Egg, (2) Nymph, (3) Emerger, (4) Dun, and (5) Adult/Spinner.

Mayflies are an important because they are found in almost all fresh water and are a large food source.

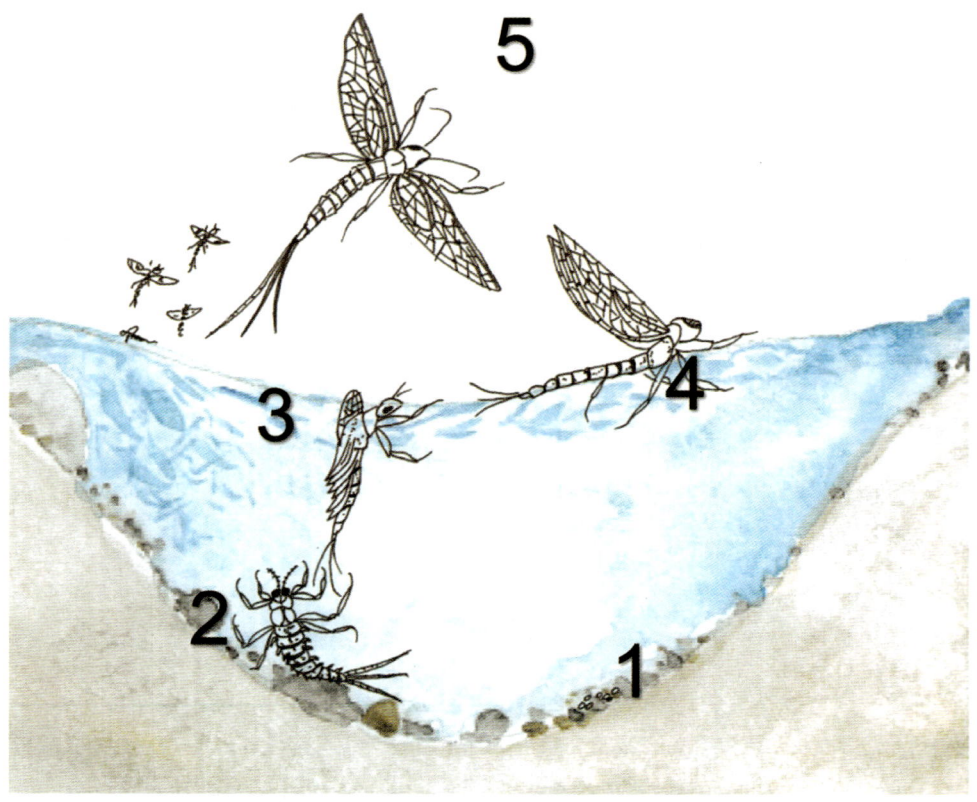

Stage 1 Eggs: Eggs are too small to be a food source for fish and sink to bottom after being laid by adults over or on the water's surface.

INSECTS AND IMITATION

Stage 2 Nymph: Nymphs are the juvenile underwater stage and have a hard exoskeleton shed several times as it grows, usually have 3 tails, long antennae, and 4-9 pairs of fan-like gills along sides. They live in weed beds, in the riverbed, and under/or rocks or timber. There are 4 basic types of Mayfly nymphs: Burrowers who dig into ground where they live most of the time, Swimmers who move like bullets (even upstream against current), Clingers who are flat with strong legs and claws, and Crawlers who crawl on bottom or on rocks.

Stage 3 Emerger/Dun: At this stage, the insect sheds its hard exoskeleton with a wing case (above thorax) to reveal wings as it emerges up to the surface to dry its wings before flying away to nearby tree limb or bush to mature and mate. This is one of most vulnerable stages to fish because the insect must rise to surface to dry wings before it can fly away. Some have difficulty puncturing through the surface film of the water and drift for longer periods of times making them even more vulnerable. They look like tiny sailboats on the surface.

Stage 5 Spinner (**Adult**): During this final stage, the insect flies out of the water once its wings are dry to a nearby tree or bush, sheds its skin again, and becomes a mature adult. It has clear wings and a colorful soft body. Adults have no working mouth parts and only live for about 24 hours during which they mate and die. The male fertilizes the female's eggs above the water and the female deposits its eggs either just above the water or by dipping her abdomen several times below the surface releasing her eggs. This is also a time when the insect is vulnerable to fish. The males and females die after shortly after mating and fall onto the water's surface often with its wings outstretched and spin in the current (known as spinners).

Some patterns that imitate the Mayfly include Nymphs: Pheasant Tail Nymph, Hares Ear Nymph, Prince Nymph, Gray Warrior, and Copper John. Adults: Adams (various colors), Blue Winged olive, Green Drake, and Gray Wulff.

INSECTS AND IMITATION

MIDGES

Diptera (DIP – TUR – UH - means two-winged)

A Midge matures in 4 stages: (1) Egg, (2) Larva, (3) Pupa, and (4) Adult with stages 2 - 4 being the most important stages. Midges are important because they are available for fish to eat all year long, often hatch where no other insects can live, and hatch in abundance which makes up for what they lack in size.

Stage 1 Egg: Eggs are too small to be a food source for fish.

Stage 2 Larvae: Small red, brown, black, or olive colored worm-like appearance and either swim or burrow in the riverbed until dislodged when you wade or by the current.

Stage 3: Pupae: Have short, segmented bodies with a thorax that contains its wings. They usually emerge in quieter sections of the water and drift on the surface (usually in groups hanging horizontally) before shedding their skin and flying away. They have a pronounced thorax, wing pads, and legs, and some live in cocoons while others grow in hardened skin shells. They rise to surface to shed their skin and drift on current until the wings dry and it can fly away.

Stage 4 Adult: The mature adult has 2 wings, fuzzy antenna and are similar looking to mosquitoes. They are sometimes difficult to see because of their small size.

Some patterns that imitate the Midge include Larvae: Zebra Midge (various colors), CDC Midge, Bead Head Worm (red), San Juan Worm, and Crystal Midge. Adults: Adams Adult, CDC Adult, Griffiths Gnat, Parachute Adams and Para Midge.

INSECTS AND IMITATION

STONEFLIES

Plecoptera (PLAY-COP-TUR-UH - Means pleated wing)

Stoneflies mature in 3 stages: (1) Egg, (2) Nymph and (3) Adult with stages 2 & 3 being the most important stages for fish and for fly fishers to learn to imitate. Stoneflies are important because they are one of the largest size flies and provide an excellent meal for fish. They are most plentiful in the summer months.

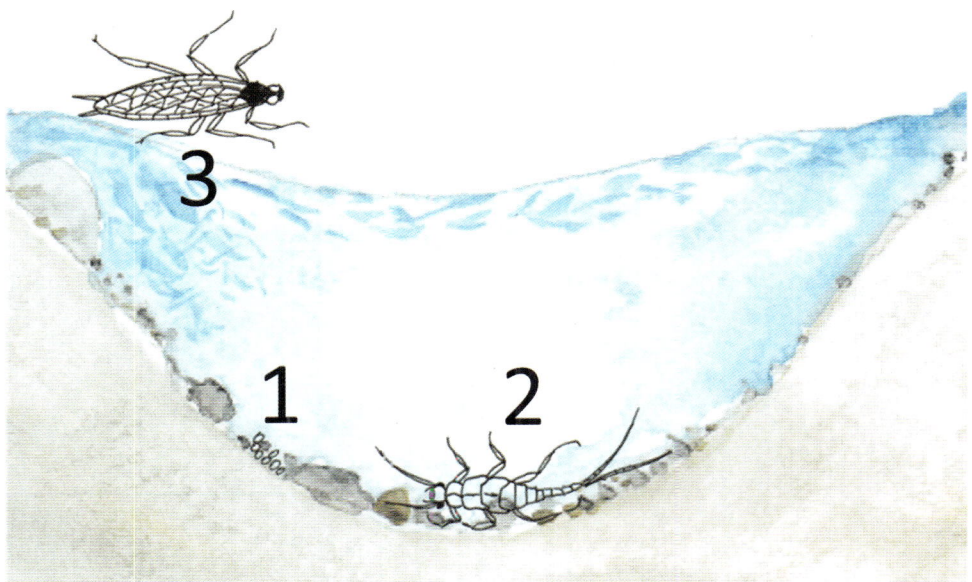

Stage 1 Egg: Eggs are too small to be a food source for fish.

Stage 2 Nymph: Stonefly nymphs are larger compared to other species of insects. They live mostly in clean, cold, and fast water, have strong legs, flat bodies that help them cling and crawl on rocks, have two tails, long antennae, and mature out of the water by crawling out onto stream side debris and rocks where they are not vulnerable to fish.

Stage 3 Adult: Adults mature out of the water away from fish. They carry 4 wings flat on back extended over the body. Stoneflies return to the water to deposit their eggs above the surface of the water or in the water like mayflies. They are clumsy flyers and often fall or get blown into the water.

Some patterns that imitate the Stonefly include Nymphs: Prince Nymph, Stonefly Nymph, Psycho Prince, and Copper john Bead Head. Adults: Golden Stonefly, Girdle Bug, Stimulator (various colors), and Rubber Leg Stonefly.

INSECTS AND IMITATION

CADDISFLIES

Trichoptera (TRY - COP - TUR – UH - Means hair winged)

Caddisflies mature in 4 stages: (1) Egg, (2) Larva, (3) Pupae and (4) Adult.

Stages 2 - 4 are the most important stages for fish and for fly fishers to learn to imitate. Caddis are important because they can be as plentiful as Mayflies and are usually available as a food source from late spring.

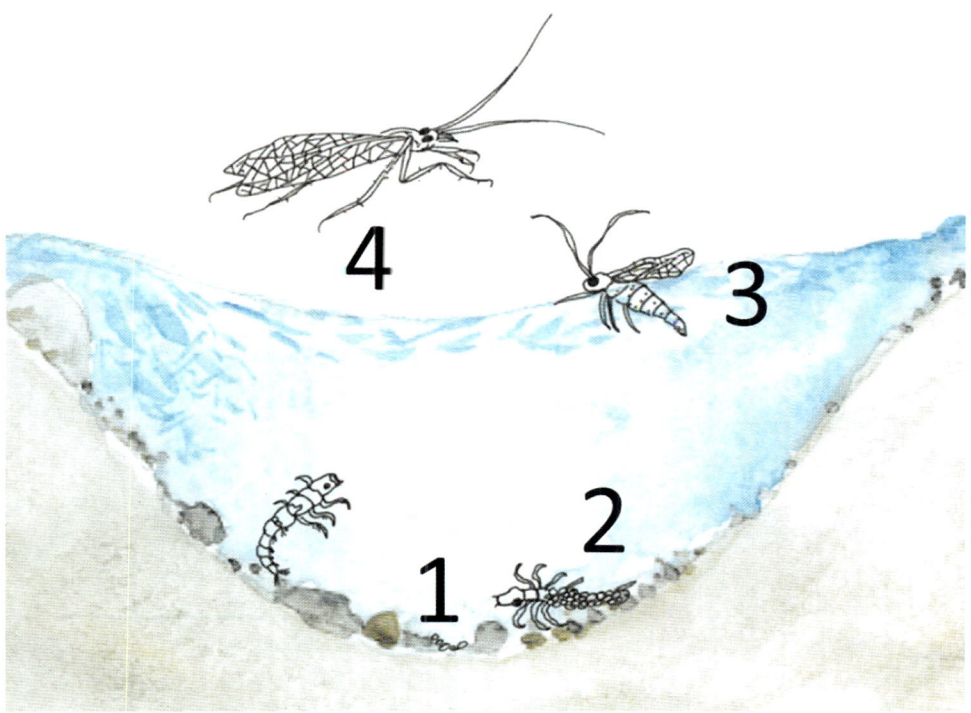

Stage 1 Egg: Eggs are too small to be a food source for fish and to imitate.

Stage 2 Larva: Larvae are small and worm-like in appearance, are green, or live in cases constructed from gravel and small sticks. They attach to rocks until they get washed free by the current or release their grip and drift downstream, or hold onto an underwater object until they mature into pupae in cocoons.

Stage 3 Pupae: Pupae transition into adults by rising to surface, shedding their skin, drifting, and eventually flying out of the water. Some crawl out onto debris and then fly away.

Stage 4 Adult: Adults resemble small moths and often emerge in fast part of the river where they can be less vulnerable to fish. They deposit eggs by flying low over the water and periodically dipping abdomen in the water and releasing eggs in a skittering motion, landing on the surface, drifting on surface, or by laying eggs on plants hanging over the water. The rain washes the eggs into water.

INSECTS AND IMITATION

Some patterns that imitate the Caddisfly include Larvae: Hares Ear Gold Rib, Green Sedge Pupa, Cased Caddis Bead Head, Caddis Pupa (brown or olive), and Caddis Emerger. Adults: CDC Caddis, Elk Hair Caddis, Hemingway Caddis, Soft Hackle Bead Head, and Klinkhamer Special.

OTHER FOOD SOURCES

DAMSELFLIES AND DRAGONFLIES

- Closely related to each other.
- The nymphs are available all year and move in short bursts.
- The adults are most plentiful in the summer, crawl out of the water to mature, and are vulnerable to fish when they chase other insects near the surface of the water.

TERRESTRIALS

- Grasshoppers, ants, beetles, etc.
- Live on land but are often blown into the water
- Plentiful in the warmer months and usually larger in size

CRUSTACEANS

- Shrimp, scuds, sowbugs, crayfish, etc.
- A scud has a small, segmented body and 7 pairs of legs, and are free swimming
- Sowbugs are also small and crawl on the bottom and hide under rocks
- Crayfish prefer warmer water and thrive on the bottom

OTHERS

- Leeches live in a variety of types of water and move slowly and are a great meal for fish
- Sculpins and other small baitfish also make tasty meals for fish
- Mice, frogs, etc.

REMEMBER:

Trout mostly eat insects that live below the surface of the water

IMMITATION FLIES

Imitation flies can be divided into 2 basic categories:

> **Dry:** Imitation flies that imitate aquatic insects, terrestrials, amphibians, mice, etc. that freely drift, swim, or float dead on or in the surface of the water. Dry flies are usually dead drifted drag free on the surface of the water but can also be animated using various techniques like skating (covered later in this guide). They are tied with materials and techniques that make them buoyant and float on the surface of the water. Dry flies can also be treated with chemicals to help hey stay afloat or you can dry your dry fly by using a technique called false casting (covered later in this book). The only weight of a dry fly is the hook and the materials it is made from.

> **Wet:** Flies that imitate insects and baitfish that live, drift, swim, or have drowned and float beneath the surface of the water. 80% of what fish eat (especially trout) live beneath the surface of the water so wet flies are important to fly fishers. Wet flies can be presented at all levels of the water column and are sometimes animated to imitate the natural behavior of the insects they are pretending to represent. Wet flies are tied with materials that help them sink. Wet flies incorporate weight that is wrapped around the shank of the hook and hidden under the body materials or use a metal bead or cone at the head of the fly.

Your main goal with either a dry or wet fly is to make it act like the insect or food the fish are eating and you are trying to imitate. If you are not able to determine what the fish are eating at the time you are fishing, then you can use the information from a hatch chart or use flies (like Wooly Buggers) to "search" for fish.

CHOOSING THE RIGHT FLY

Choosing the right fly to use is not always easy which is what I find interesting and challenging about fly fishing. The illustration and questions below show you some of the factors that can help you choose a fly that will give you the best chance at catching fish.

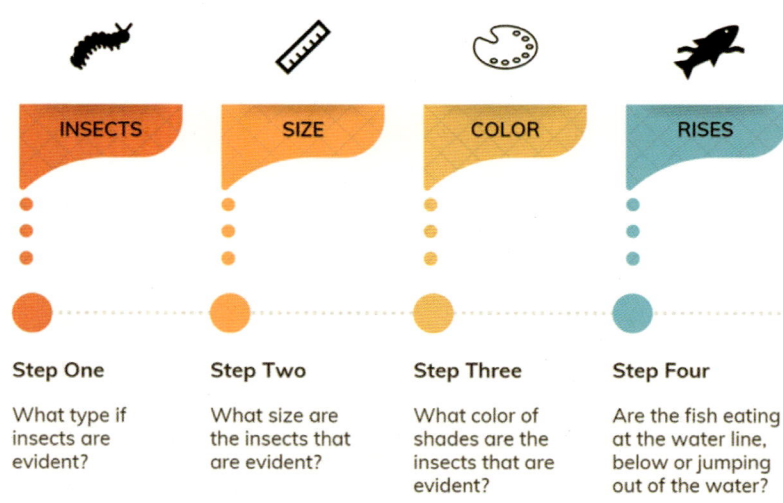

Step One — What type if insects are evident?

Step Two — What size are the insects that are evident?

Step Three — What color of shades are the insects that are evident?

Step Four — Are the fish eating at the water line, below or jumping out of the water?

INSECTS AND IMITATION

Insects: Can you see what fish are eating. Can you scoop up a handful of gravel from the bottom of the river and see what type of insects are present? You can purchase a small seine net or glove that you can use for this purpose. What type of insects are native to the area where you are fishing? Is there a hatch chart available? Is there a fly shop nearby that you can visit and ask what is hatching and what type of flies are catching fish? If you are not able to see or find any insects, then you can try using a search or exploring pattern of fly.

Size: What size insects are present? Try and match the size of the insects present to the size of the hook for the fly pattern you are selecting. You will want to have various sizes of most flies in your fly box so that you can match the size of the insects present. Most insects do not vary greatly in size so a few hook sizes up and down should suffice.

Color: What color are the insects that are present? Try and match their natural color to the type of fly pattern you choose. Try and carry a few different colors of the same fly pattern.

Rises: Can you see fish feeding in a specific way or pattern? Sometimes you will get a hint of what fish are eating and what fly to use by the way fish are feeding (refer to rise forms later in this book for more information).

CHOOSING THE RIGHT FLY

Fly Fishing Journal

BEFORE YOU ARRIVE AT THE RIVER

- ☐ Find ways to familiarize yourself with the river you are going to fish.
- ☐ Search for a hatch chart specific to the river you will fish.
- ☐ Find a local fly fishing shop near the river and visit it before you fish to see what insects are hatching and what flies are being used as imitations.
- ☐ Ask about the river in one of the many fly fishing groups online.
- ☐ Make sure you have the sizes, colors, and lifecycle flies in your

WHEN YOU ARRIVE AT THE RIVER

- ☐ Identify areas where fish may be holding and where you will enter the river to get to the spot you selected with as much stealth as possible.
- ☐ Are there fast and slow currents that you will need to cast across causing your fly and line to drift at 2 different speeds forcing you to have to make corrections?
- ☐ Can you see any fish? If yes, how are they behaving? Are they rising to the surface to eat, or do you see tails breaking the surface indicating they are feeding on insects below the surface?
- ☐ Can you find any insects present in the water, under rocks, in the gravel of the riverbed, or in the bushes or spider webs on

AFTER YOU FISH

- ☐ Write down some observations about your experience?
  - o What flies were successful/unsuccessful and why?
  - o What corrections did you have to make (e.g., mending, etc.)
  - o Did you present your fly to fish you could see and they didn't bite? Why?
- ☐ Draw an illustration of the area your fished. Include where you entered the river, stood and the spots you targeted. Draw in the types of currents, the approximate depth of the water,

INSECTS AND IMITATION

DRY AND WET FLIES

There are different types of dry and wet flies that are named either by the person who invented the pattern or the insect they imitate.

DRY FLY TYPES

Terrestrials imitate land-based insects like ants and grasshoppers that fall or get blown into the water in warmer months. They are tied with foam and other buoyant materials.

Poppers imitate surface insects and amphibians that swim on the surface and are tied with tightly packed deer hair or foam designed to make a splash when they are retrieved.

Hackled flies are tied with hackle feathers that make the fly float high on the surface of the water.

Parachute flies have a hair wing or other material post that stands straight up in the air and remains above the surface of the water while the rest of the body drifts below the surface.

Attractor are generic and are tied with colorful and shiny materials that attract fish to strike.

WET FLY TYPES

Nymphs imitate immature insects, snails, scuds, and worms that live below the surface.

Emergers imitate hatching insects that rise toward the surface before leaving the water.

Streamers imitate swimming, injured, or fleeing baitfish or can be used to search the water.

Soft Hackle flies are sparsely tied with thread, floss, peacock hurl, and a soft hackle feather tied in at the head. The hackle suggests the legs or emergent wings.

Flymphs represent the transitional hatching stage between nymph (or pupa) and dun or adult.

Egg fly patterns are meant to imitate the spawn of other fish.

Below are some of the more popular types and sizes of dry and wet flies:

DRY FLIES
Adams (12-20)
Bivisible (12-20)
Cahill (12-20)
Elk Hair Caddis (12-24)
Royal Wulff (12-18)
Hendrickson (14-20)
Quill Gorcon (12-20)
Humphy (12-18)

TERRESTRIALS
Black Ant (14-18)
Beatle (8-14)
Hopper (2-8)
Spider (8-14)

NYMPHS
Gold Ribbed Hares Ear (10-16)
Hares Ear (10-16)
Prince Nymph (10-14)
Caddis Pupa (12-16)
Caddis Larva (12-16)
Zug Bug (12-16)

STREAMERS
Muddler Minnow (4-12)
Light/Dark Spruce (4-8)
Black Marabou (4-8)
Wooly Bugger (2-8)
Clouser Minnor (2-8)

ORGANIZING YOUR FLIES

There are many ways to store, organize, and carry your flies and it may take you a while before you find a method that works best for you. It's important to carry the types of flies that best imitate the insects that are available to fish in the specific river or stream where you plan to fish at that specific time of the year. I also carry in my box a few generic and/or search pattern types of flies that imitate an array of insects.

Fly fishing is different from spin fishing where you carry all your gear in as large of a tackle box as you can afford. Fly fishers carry all their equipment on them so it's important to carry only the essential equipment you will need and to make sure your fishing vest or pack can fit everything.

Your choice of fly boxes is important. A quality fly box will store your flies, protect them from the elements, and keep them from falling into the water and drifting away. You also want a box that is big enough to hold your largest fly (unless you will sort your flies into different boxes). Flies are usually held in place inside the box by foam (sometimes the smallest flies can be held

INSECTS AND IMITATION

magnetically) but manufacturers are experimenting with different materials all the time. Purchase a box that makes it easy for you to get your flies in and out of the box and hold all of the flies you feel you need that day when you fish.

Flies can be organized in several different ways:

BY TYPE/PATTERN:
Dry flies, wet flies, nymphs, midges, streamers, etc.

BY INSECT:
According to the insects and their life cycles (e.g., Mayfly nymphs, emergers, duns, etc. that live in the specific rivers or streams where you plan to fish

BY SIZE
#12 Parachute Adams, #20 Parachute Adams, #12 Hares Ear Tan, #12 Hares Ear Black, etc.

BY SEASON
Fall, spring, summer, and winter. You can take out and put the flies in as the seasons change

I keep a large fly box at home that contains all the flies I use and then pick from that selection depending on the season, the type of fish I am trying to catch, and/or the location of the river and put them into a smaller box.

DRY AND WET FLIES | 69

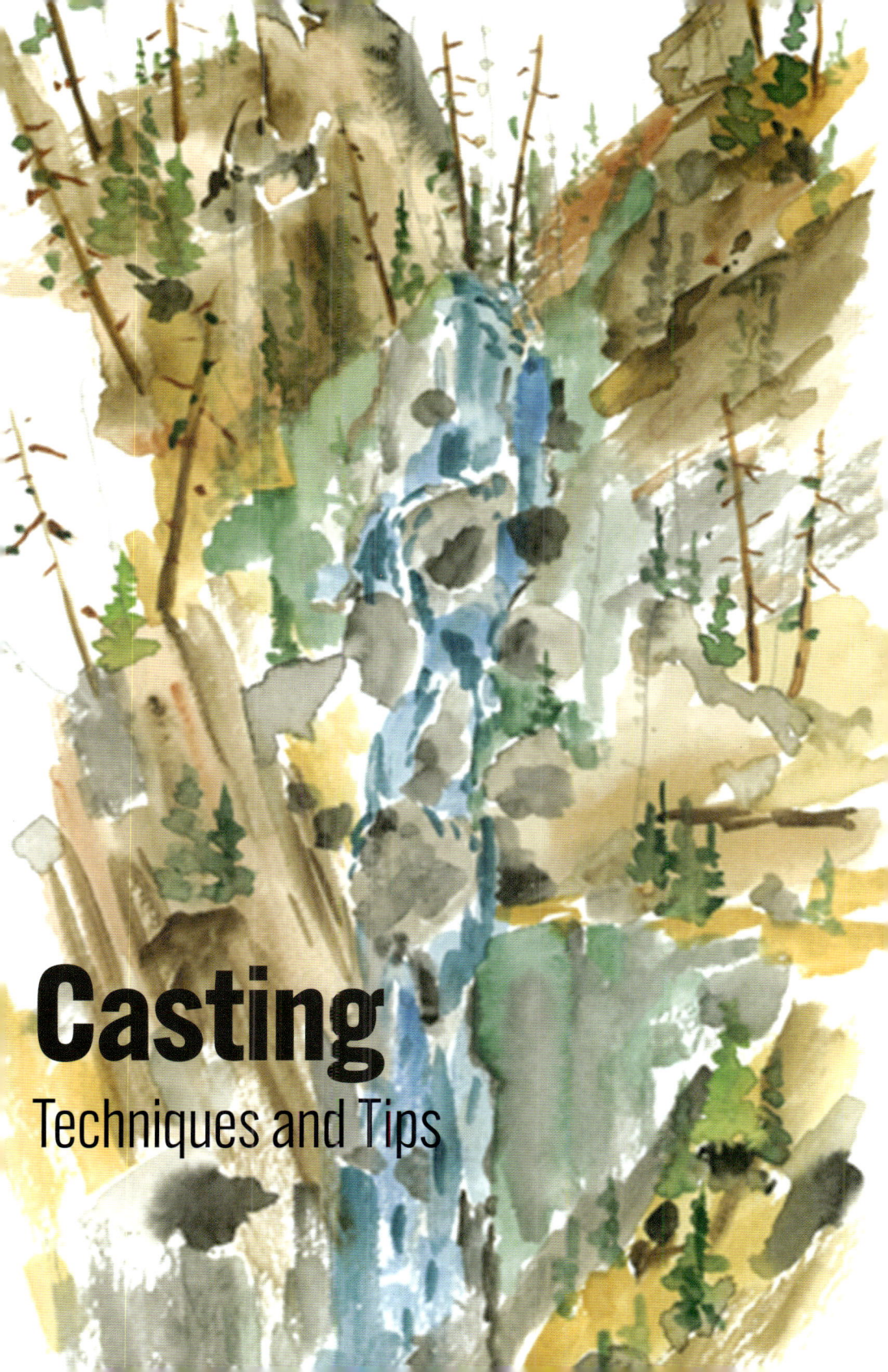

Casting
Techniques and Tips

ROD GRIPS

There are a few different types of ways to hold a fly rod. My advice is to try them out and see which one feels most comfortable to you.

Thumb on Top Grip – This is one of the most popular grips and the one I use. This grip provides me with comfort and helps me make accurate and effective casts.

STEPS:

1. Place your thumb extended over the top of the rod's cork grip.
2. Place your index finger underneath your thumb with the remaining fingers lending support by gripping the cork handle.
3. Your thumb should be pointing at your target at the end of your forward cast. This helps avoid tailing loops (when the top part of the line hits the bottom).
4. The rod should remain close to or against your wrist.

CASTING

Index Finger on Top Grip - Some people prefer this grip because they can hold the line with their middle finger and get a better feel for each cast. Can be used for soft, delicate casts.

STEPS:

1. Pointing your index finger straight ahead along the handle.
2. Point your rod straight ahead and parallel to the ground.
3. The rod should remain close to or against your wrist.

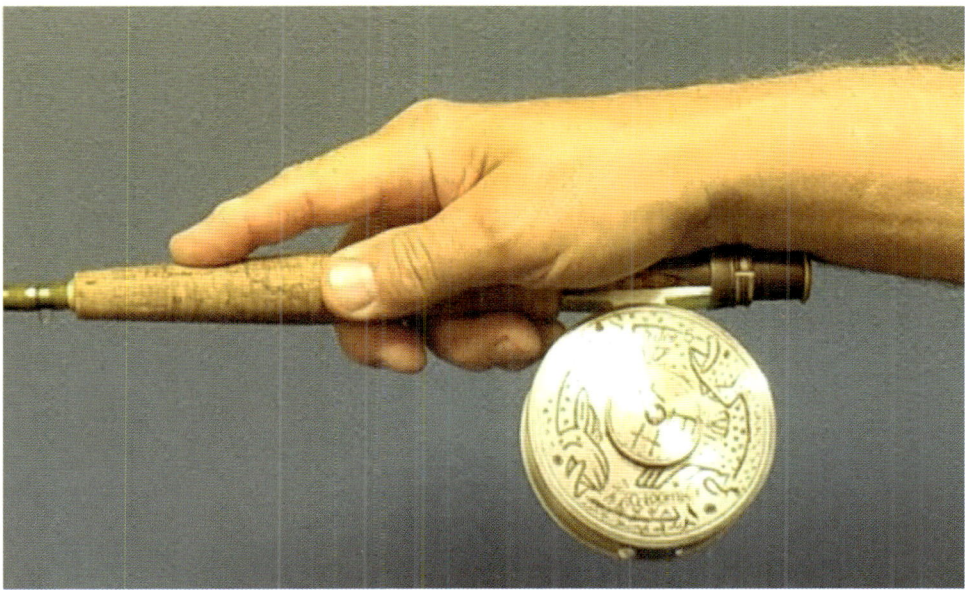

This grip allows the rod to be an extension of your index finger so you can point in the direction of the target. This ensures that the rod will be traveling in the same direction as your line.

LINE HAND & WRIST

LINE HAND

Your line hand is used to control your line and sometimes help set the hook when a strike occurs. Your line should rest securely across the four fingers of your line hand and under your thumb with your hand always closed prepared to stop of release the line when needed. Some people use their thumb and index finger instead of all of their fingers.

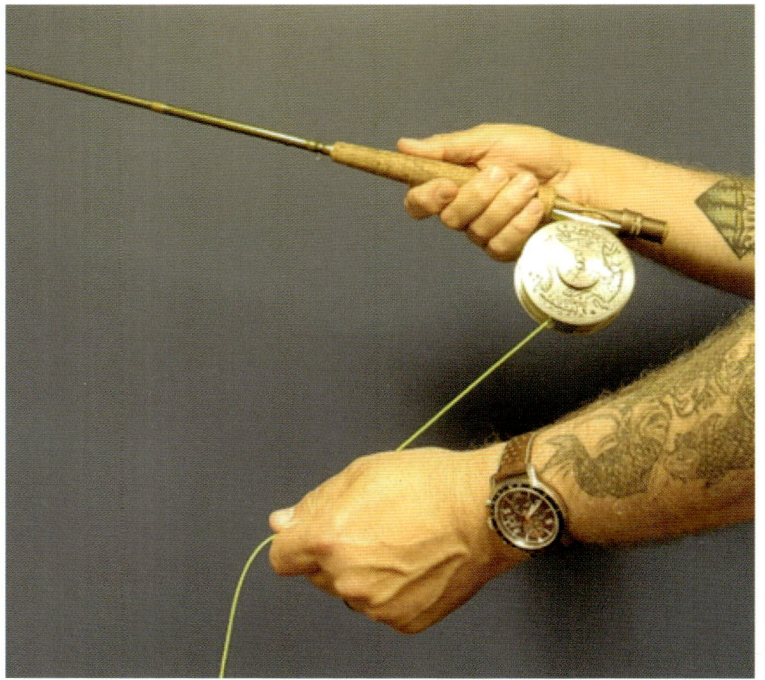

CASTING

THE WRIST

Your wrist does not play a major role in casting and should remain relatively stiff and/or straight. Bending your rod hand wrist too far in any direction negatively impacts your cast. I used to tuck the butt end of my rod inside my long shirt sleeve which prevented me from bending my wrist too far when I first learned to cast. There are also devices made that attach to your rod and wrist that are helpful when you are learning to cast to help you avoid bending your wrist. Below you will see an illustration of the correct wrist position on the back cast.

STANCES

The term "casting stance" refers to the position of your feet when you cast. Below are three of the most common stances. You may not always be able to stand perfectly due rocks and other debris at the bottom of a river but always try and have a stable stance before your cast. Practice casting using various stances and positions.

OPEN STANCE

This is a popular stance because it allows you to watch and analyze your back cast without moving or turning your shoulders.

1. (Assumes you are right handed) Position your right foot back with your weight placed on this foot.
2. Position your left leg forward.
3. Your weight shifts from the back to the front with the movement of your rod as you cast.

CLOSED STANCE

This is opposite the open stance with your casting hand leg positioned forward and your line hand leg in the rear.

SQUARED STANCE

Face your target with both legs squared. Align your rod with the target and cast. This stance does not allow you to watch your back cast without turning.

THE PLANE

The casting plane is the path your rod and line travel during your cast. You want a tight loop for most of your casts. You achieve a tighter loop and more effective cast when your rod and line travel along in the same straight path. Your line always follows the path of your rod tip so if you rod tip strays outside the plane, your line will follow.

As you learn to cast you can watch your line roll out from your front or back cast. The shape of your line is called the loop. Keep in mind that you are trying to "Not" bend your arm or wrist when you cast. Think of trying to cast an apple on a stick and have the apple hit a specific target of your choice. If you move the apple on the stick back too quickly, the apple will slide off the stick and land behind you. If you start off slowly backwards and then accelerate the stick forward and abruptly stop at the right moment, you will cast the apple as far as it can go toward your target. If you don't stop the stick at a certain point and continue moving it forward, the apple will crash to the ground close to where you are standing. Fly casting is based on the same principle.

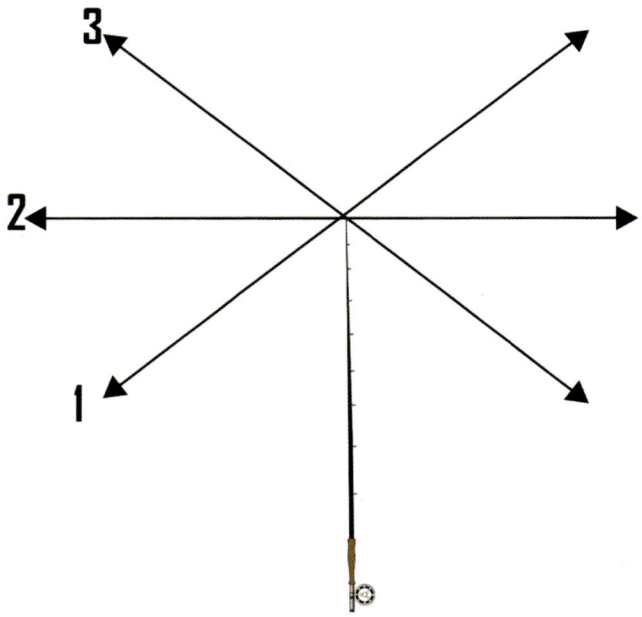

BACK CAST

The back cast is the first part of your cast. The weight of your fly line on the water combined with the acceleration of your back cast loads your rod. The weight of the line and the load of the rod varies based on the length of line extended. Smaller lengths of line create less force. Holding your rod handle close to your wrist also helps load the rod. The tip of your rod is what travels along the casting plane. Make sure that your rod tips travels in the same horizontal and vertical casting plane. You do not want to alter the casting plane once you start your cast because that will negatively impact the effectiveness and accuracy of your cast.

STEPS:

1. Begin with your rod butt as close to your wrist as possible (1).
2. Start a slow acceleration backwards and remove as much of your line off the water as possible. Keep your wrist still or locked and the rod handle close to or against your wrist (2).
3. Proceed to a fast and smooth acceleration of the rod and line backward building to a speed up and stop at between 12 and 1 o'clock (3).

Practice making your rod tip travel in the same vertical and horizontal plane and remember that your line needs to just about straighten out before you begin your forward cast (3).

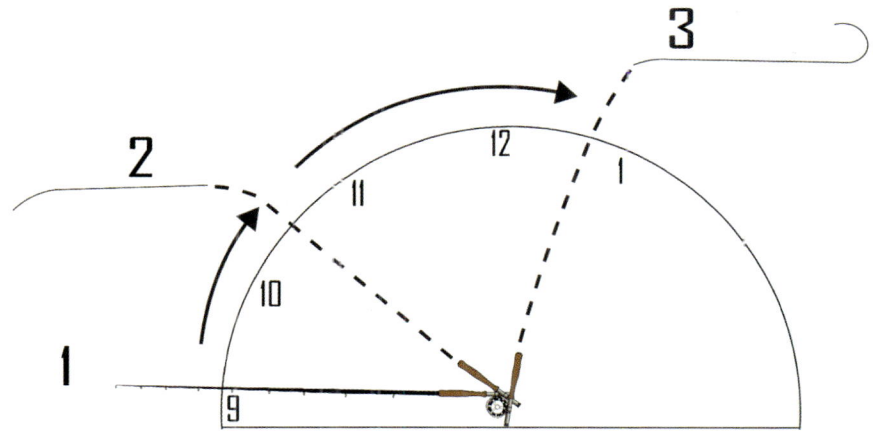

FORWARD CAST

The forward cast in the second part of your cast that also loads the rod and propels your line and fly forward to your target. This part of the cast controls accuracy.

STEPS:

1. The forward cast begins when your line has just about straightened out at the end of your back cast leaving a small tight loop (1). Keep in mind that you are "pushing" your wrist and thumb toward your target. The wrist does not really play a major role in the cast so keep it as straight as possible. Think of the forward cast like flicking paint off a brush or an apple off a stick.
2. Push your cast forward from your shoulder with your forearm and elbow speeding up and stopping the acceleration of the rod to load between 11 and 10 o'clock (2).
3. Let your line loop form and the line straighten out in front of you before you slowly lower the rod toward the water and begin your presentation (3).

Most of the times you want to avoid making your fly "slap" and slash on the surface of the water unless that is a technique you are trying to achieve (like a frog jumping off a bank into the water) or you are trying to drive your wet fly down deeper into the water where fish are holding that won't be frightened by the initial splash of your fly on the surface of the water.

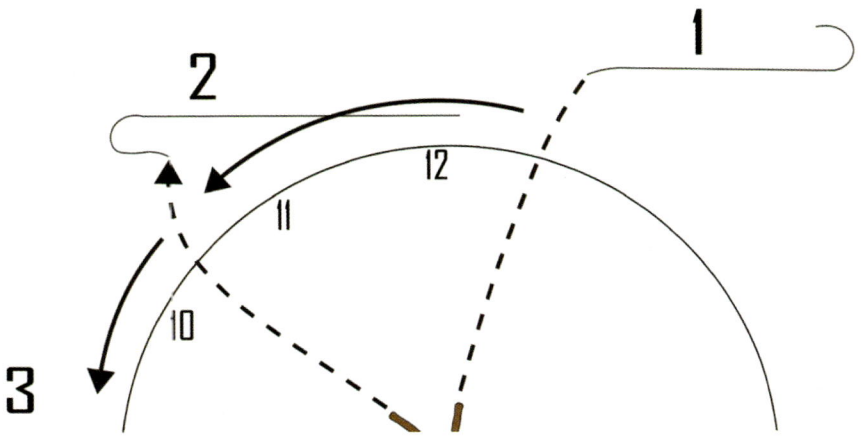

CASTING

LOOPS

A casting loop refers to the distance between the top and bottom of your fly line during your casting stroke. You are usually trying to achieve tight loops that are approximately 1-2 feet apart to maximize the load of your rod and to make as an effective and accurate cast as possible.

Loop size is determined by the position of your rod tip relative to the path of your fly line at the completion of your forward casting stoke. Your casting loop begins to form when your line passes over the rod tip where the other end of the line is anchored. If you stop your rod tip high (usually between 10-11 o'clock) and just below the fly line as it moves forward, you will achieve a tight loop. The farther your rod tip travels and stops, the more open your loop will be. We use different types of loops for different casting situations. For example, a tight loop helps you to cast farther or shoot your line under trees (a sidearm cast can also be used). A more open loop is better for heaver weighted flies, when you are using a sink tip (which adds weight to your line, or on windy days. Practice achieving different size loops and practice casting on windy days.

TIGHT LOOPS

A tight casting loop is preferred for most fly fishing situations. Tight loops are more efficient for moving your line through the air, transferring the energy in the line, and for giving you a longer and more accurate cast. Tight loops penetrate the wind better and have greater line speed because the loop is smaller. You will not throw a tight loop if you end your forward stroke too low, break your wrist, or do not accelerate your rod tip along a straight plane throughout the entire casting arc.

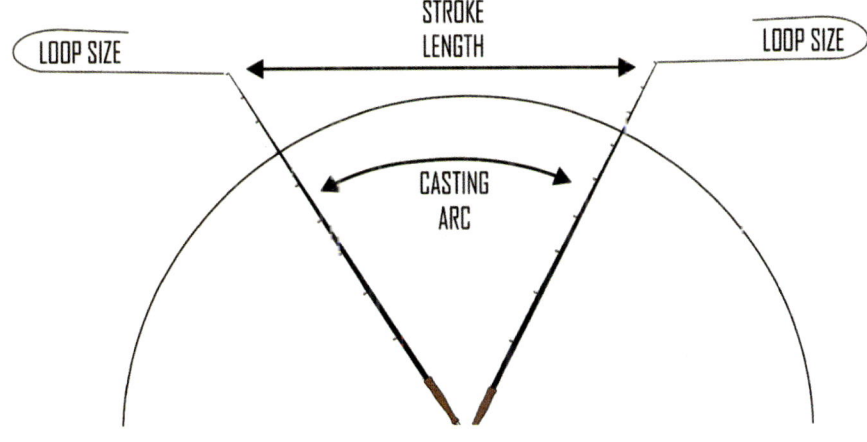

OPEN AND WIDE LOOPS

You usually use a tight and closed loop when you cast but there are times when an open or wide loop comes in handy. Open or wide loops are useful if you are using a sink tip/sinking that adds additional weight to your line or if you are using heavily weighted flies.

One of the main ways to throw a more open or wide loop is to increase the length of your casting arc by letting your rod travel in a wider casting arc than normal. Instead of stopping your back cast between 12 and 1 o'clock and your forward cast between 10-11 o'clock, stop your back cast at approximately 1-2 o'clock and your forward cast between 9-10 o'clock. In other words, lengthen both your back and forward cast. Being able to cast and control your loop size is a good skill to practice and master.

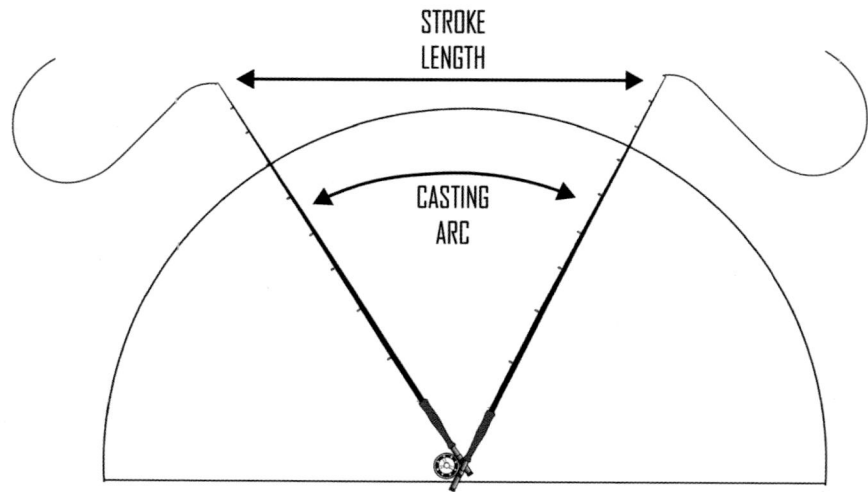

FALSE CASTING

The false cast is a series of back and forward casts without ever completing the cast and letting the line or fly touch down on the water until your final forward cast when you release the line and complete the cast. False casts are used to dry your fly, judge the distance to a target, change your casting direction between casts, add line into your cast, shoot line for longer casts, and/or to bring your line in closer.

STEPS:

1. Make your regular back cast
2. Make your regular forward cast but do not release the line
3. Repeat steps 1 and 2
4. Release your line when you are ready

False casting is a great way to practice and analyze your cast. Find yourself a long patch of grass and practice false casting to fine tune your timing, get the feel for when to start your forward cast, experiment with rod angles and stroke lengths, and improve the size of your casting loops.

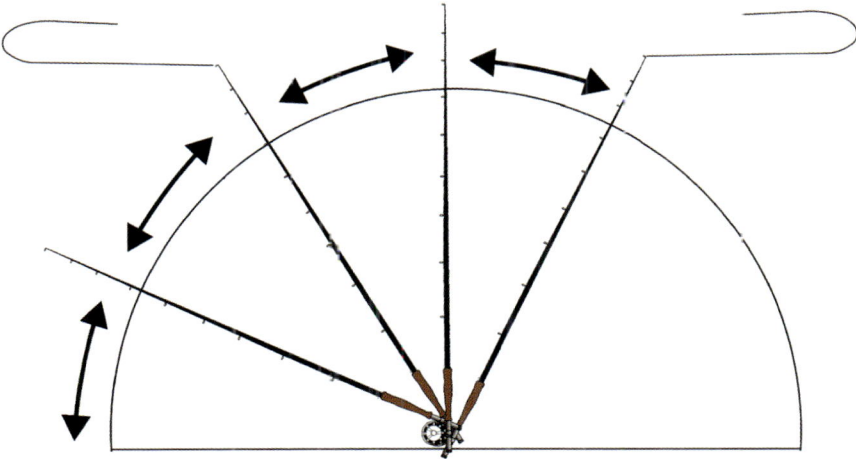

CASTING DRIFT

Casting drift is a technique that is used to lengthen your casting stroke or arc for the purposes of making a longer cast or to remove excess energy in the rod tip to achieve a smoother and more accurate cast. It is a slight (2-3 inch) backward drift of your rod hand at the completion of your back cast.

STEPS:

1. Make your regular back cast.
2. Before you complete your back cast and your speed-up-and-stop, let your entire rod (not just the tip) drift backwards (approximately 3 inches) and slightly upward along the same path as your line unrolls. Do not bend your wrist, tilt the rod tip backwards, or let your casting arm drift downwards
3. Make your regular forward cast..

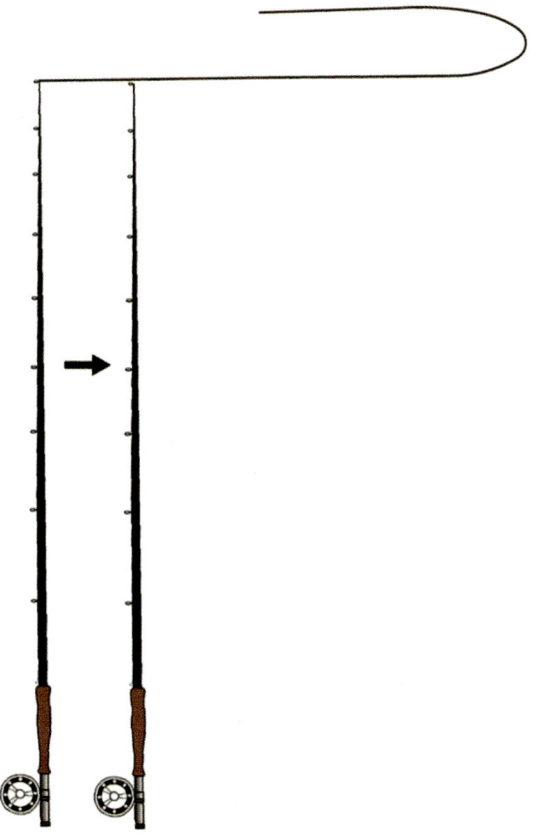

CASTING

TUCK/TUG CAST

The Tuck/Tug Cast can be used to sink a wet fly more quickly. The tug/tuck at the completion of the cast helps drive your fly downward faster toward the surface of the water and puts a length of slack on the water at the conclusion of the cast. This cast is merely an overpowered and high regular forward cast.

STEPS:

1. Make a regular back cast (1).
2. Make a faster and higher than average forward cast overshooting your target (2). The higher the stop, the greater the tug on the fly downward. You are overshooting your target because the tug/tuck at the end of your forward cast will pull in a length of line and should allow your fly to land ahead of your target area. You also do not have to cast over your target and can tug/tuck ahead of it and let your fly drift drag-free to your target area.
3. At the end of your forward cast and speed up and stop, tuck, or tug your rod backward causing the rod to slightly recoil which causes your fly to be pushed down toward the surface of the water at a faster then normal rate of speed and puts the extra line on the surface of the water to avoid drag early on in your presentation (3).
4. Lower your rod tip as your line and leader pile up on the water.

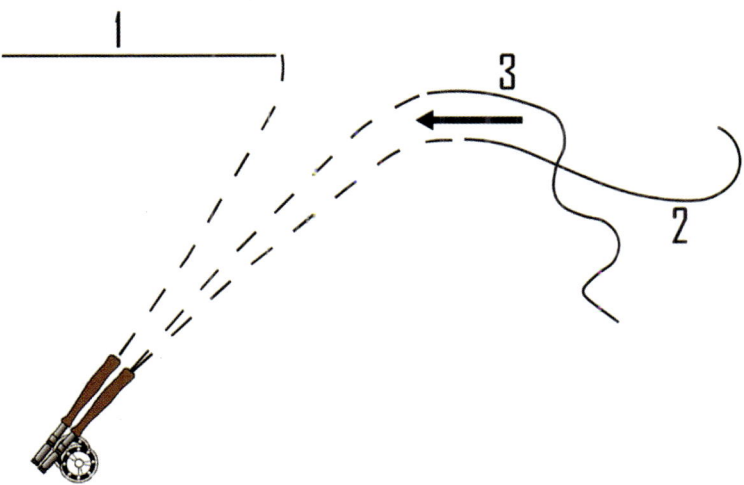

ROLL CAST

The Roll Cast is used when there are obstructions behind you (trees, bushes, etc.) preventing you from making your regular back cast. The roll cast uses the force of the grip of the water on your line to build momentum and load your rod to make your forward cast. This is a cast that needs to be practiced on water. It is a very worthwhile cast to master and will come in handy when you are trying to fish from the banks of a river or lake that has a lot of trees or bushes on the banks.

STEPS:

1. Accelerate your rod back slowly (1 & 2) and smoothly past your regular back cast position (3) until a "D" loop forms in the line behind you.
2. When your line stops moving and while it is still gripped by the water, cast the line forward with a short, smooth, speed-up-and-stop (4). This creates the loop that unrolls out onto the water and flips your fly forward.

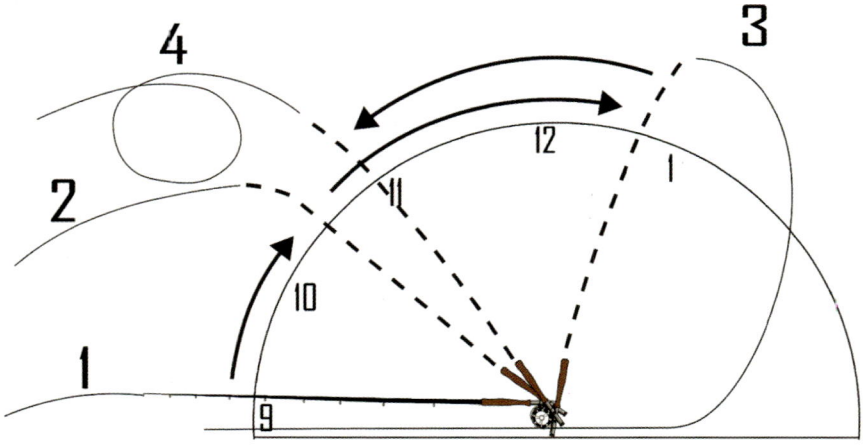

PARACHUTE CAST

The Parachute Cast (like the tuck/tug cast) is used when you need to land your fly softly on the surface. An added benefit is that this type of cast also usually results in some line slack on the water at the end of your cast. I like to use this cast to present some types of dry flies that imitate dead insects falling on to the surface of the water. It is a cast that is good to use to present a fly downstream because of the slack on the water that will help avoid drag at the start of your presentation.

STEPS:

1. Make your regular back cast (1).
2. End your forward cast at a higher than normal point. At the end of your forward cast stop, don't lower your rod tip toward the surface of the water. This makes your fly float down onto the surface of the water with a soft landing (2).
3. As the line straightens out, your fly will drift softly to the surface of the water with enough slack to avoid drag from occurring at the conclusion of your cast. Once you fly is on the surface (or close to) you can lower your rod tip.

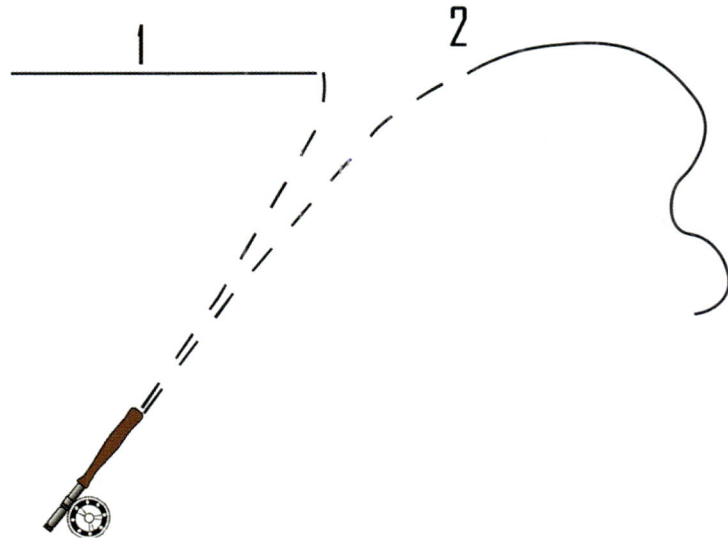

SLACK, S, or SERPENTINE CAST

The Slack, S, or Serpentine Cast is a simple yet effective cast that puts slack on the water at the conclusion of your forward cast. It requires you to wiggle your rod tip at the completion of your forward cast. This causes your line to fall on the water in a series of "S" shaped curves.

STEPS:

1. Make your regular forward cast and stop slightly higher than normal. Make sure that you have a length of additional line stripped off your reel and in your line hand.
2. While your forward cast is still in the air, shake your rod tip side to side (approximately 5-6 inches) side to side as you lower your rod toward the surface of the water. The shaking movement causes extra line (S curves) to form in the line and slack to fall on the water at the conclusion of your cast. Don't shake your rod tip too much to cause a redirection of your fly in the air. By shaking your rod tip, you are merely releasing extra line slack into your cast at the end.

Keep in mind that the "S" curves will shorten your cast, so you need to compensate in relation to the distance to your target.

REACH CAST

The Reach Cast is another type of cast that puts slack on the water at the end of your cast. It involves a type of "aerial" mend.

STEPS:

1. End your forward cast with your rod tip slightly higher (between 11 -12 o'clock) (1).
2. Reach your rod arm upstream (approximately 4-5 inches) just before your line lands on the water. This "reach" puts slack immediately on the water.

The most effective reaches are completed when your line is still shooting forward and just before your it lands on the water. If you reach and lay your fly line at an upstream angle it should give your fly a longer drag-free drift.

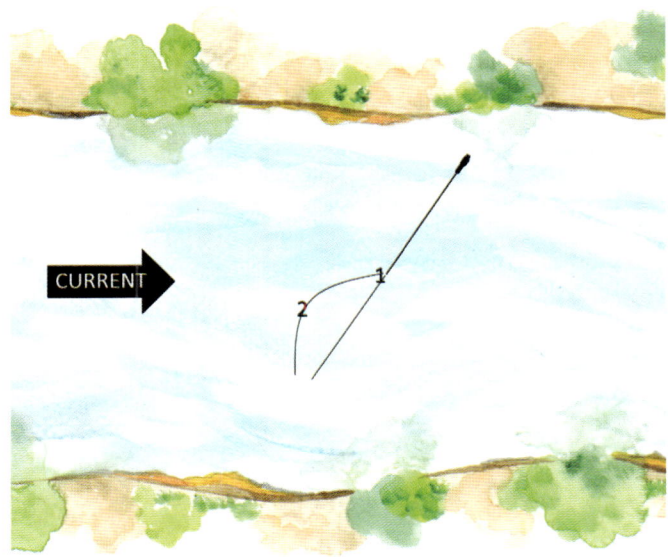

SIDE ARM CAST

The Side Arm Cast is useful in windy conditions because there is usually less wind current near the surface of the water than higher up in the air where your line travels during your regular cast. This cast also is also useful for avoiding obstructions like trees that may overhang the bank. The side arm cast uses the same basic casting principles as your overhead cast with the exception that 12 o'clock is moved straight out to your side parallel to the water or ground. Don't let your rod travel to close to the surface of the water or the end of your line or fly may dip into the water and negatively impact the load of your rod and your casting accuracy. I usually keep my casting arm slightly above my waste unless I am standing in deeper water and need to adjust my arm higher.

STEPS:

1. Use your regular casting stroke only with your rod on an even and parallel plane with the water.
2. Your line should straighten out behind you at the end of your backstroke with the same tight loop as a regular cast. Don't let your rod tip travel too far back in the casting arc or it will negatively impact your loop and forward cast.

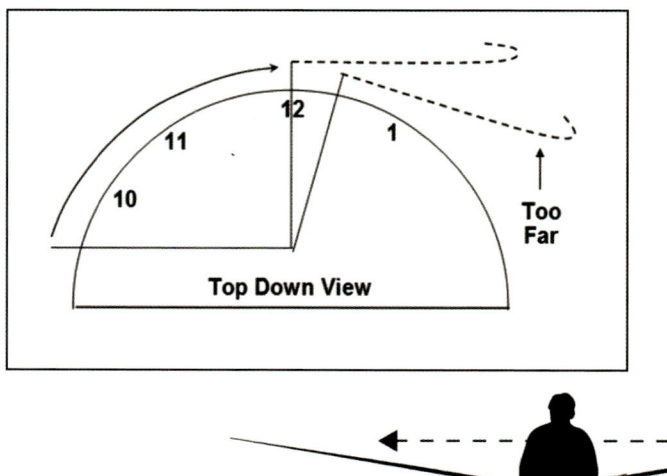

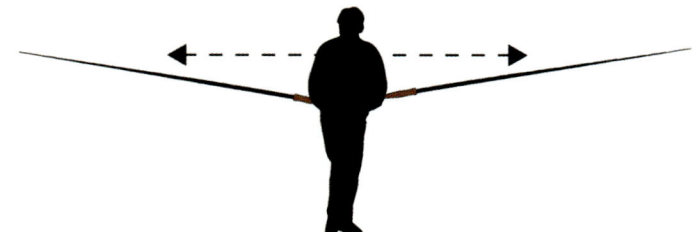

WIND Casting

Wind makes it more difficult to cast because of the limited weight of the fly line so it is important to learn some basic strategies to combat the impact of the wind on your cast.

- A Side Arm Cast is helpful on windy days because your forward and back cast travel closer to the surface of the water where there is usually less wind resistance.
- Make your casting loops as tight as possible and speed up your line speed
- Tilt your cast slightly downward (see illustration below) and stop your forward cast between 9 and 10 o'clock as opposed to 10-11 o'clock.
- Heavier weight rods are better in windy conditions.
- Reposition yourself so that the wind aids your forward cast.
- Make your line slice through the wind faster with a double haul.
- Reduce the number of false casts.

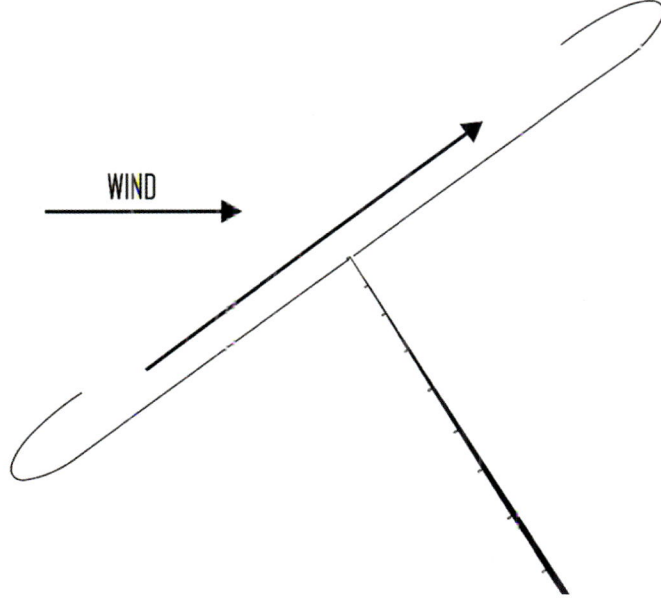

DRAG

WHAT IS DRAG?

The term "drag" refers to the unnatural pull on your fly from your fly line. Drag is easily detected by fish and will usually cause the fish to refuse your fly because it is not behaving like the real insect or baitfish it is used to seeing and eating (when was the last time you saw an insect being dragged down the river by a line?).

Drag is caused when your fly line and fly travel and/or drift down the river or stream at a different rate of speed. The current of a river is not all flowing at the same pace. The current on the surface travels faster than the current in the middle and at the bottom of the water or the current closest to you may be faster than the current where your fly lands in the water. For example, if you are using a floating line with a wet fly, the current may pull your line downstream faster than the slower current below the surface where your wet fly is drifting. Another example is when you cast across one current into another. Your fly line then travels at a different rate of spend than your dry or wet fly. The pull of the different current on your fly line and fly causes a "belly" to form in your line that needs to be removed to avoid drag and the unnatural presentation of your fly (see the illustration below).

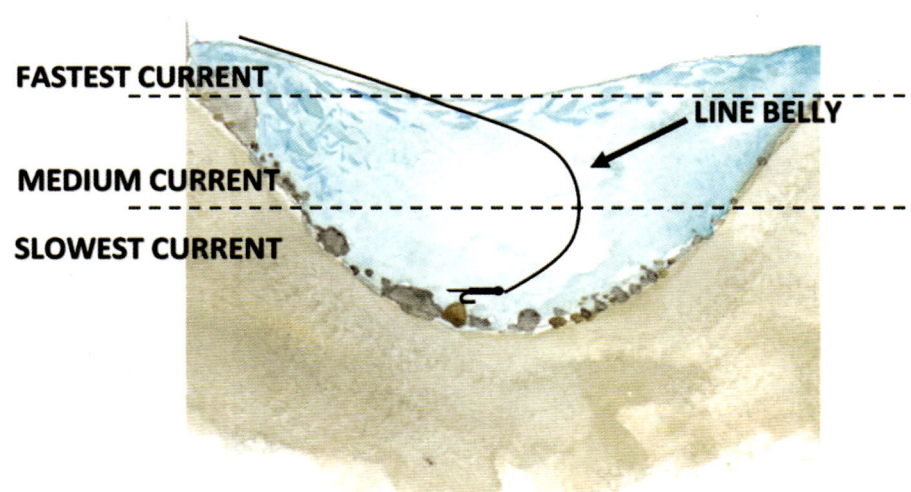

CASTING

MENDING

CONTROLLING DRAG

Learning to control and eliminate drag is one of the most important skills to master because you will need to control your line as it is impacted by the current of the water. The impact of the different currents on your line and fly causes your fly act unnaturally and fish to refuse your fly.

Mending is a technique used to eliminate drag. When you mend, you intentionally reposition your fly line to eliminate the belly and drag in your line. I suggest practicing mending until you are comfortable doing it repeatedly.

When you practice mending, cast across the water, and observe the drift of your fly line as compared to your fly. Did a belly form in your line causing it to drift downstream faster that your fly? Did you fly travel downstream faster than your line and removed all the slack in your line? Make another cast and mend your line when a belly forms. Did the mend eliminate the belly and the drag in the line? Try bigger and smaller mends. Do you notice any differences? Were you able to make your fly travel downstream before your line? Before you cast you need to analyze the current and decide how to cast and control your line. I usually make a practice cast or two if I am fishing a spot that is unfamiliar to me. Below is an example of how to mend.

Cast across and slightly upstream (1). Follow your line downstream with the tip of your rod. If a downstream belly forms in your line mend upstream to eliminate the belly in the line (2 & 3). If you are using a dry fly, do not lift too much line off the water when you mend or you will also alter the path of your fly. If you are using a wet fly, you can use the mending technique to life your fly higher in the water column.

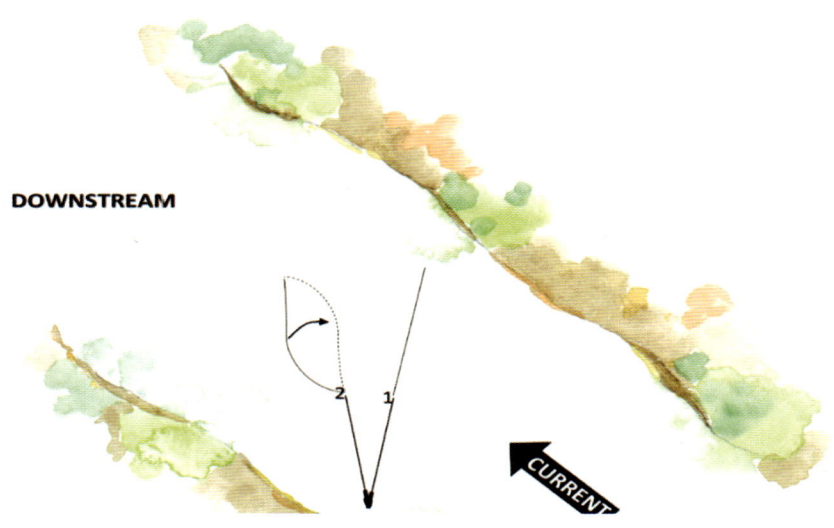

WET AND DRY FLY MENDING

Dry and wet flies are mended differently.

Dry Fly Mend: The purpose of a dry fly mend is to eliminate drag on your fly. You mend your line upstream to remove the belly caused when the current pulls your fly line downstream faster than your fly. You are trying not to move your fly, only your line.

1. Make your cast.
2. If a belly forms in your line, slightly raise your rod tip just enough to remove some line slack off the water but not too much that you pull your fly toward you.
3. With your rod tip in the air, mend (flip) your line to the opposite side of your line belly (e.g., if your line belly has formed to the right, mend to your left) to remove the belly and slack. Try not to move your fly when you mend.
4. Continue your presentation and control the slack in your line.

CASTING

Wet Fly Mend: The purpose of a wet fly mend is also to eliminate drag on your fly but also to adjust your fly to the depth where fish are feeding or to animate your fly to better imitate the insect to are trying to mimic.

1. Make your cast.
2. If you are casting across a slower current into a faster one, the tip of your fly line will drift faster than the rest of your fly line a belly will form in your line causing drag and an unnatural presentation of your fly.
3. Mend by lifting your rod and the part of your line closest to your rod off the water surface and flip your line to the left to remove the belly in your line. This is also your opportunity to adjust the depth of your fly in the water. The higher you lift your rod, the higher you fly will move toward the surface of the water to match the depth of your target fish.
4. Continue to control your line and drag.
5. Continue your presentation downstream toward your target.

The timing of when to mend is important. You want to mend well before your fly nears your target.

CASTING ACROSS A SLOWER TO FASTER CURRENT

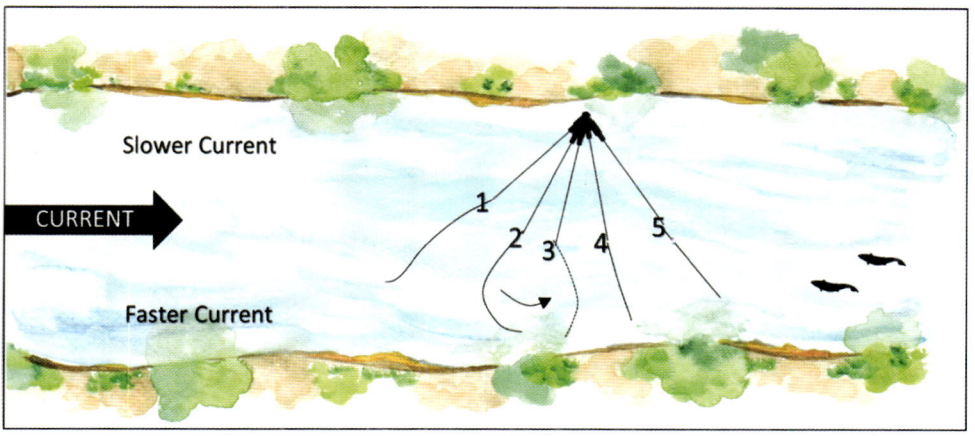

MENDING | 95

CASTING ACROSS A FASTER TO SLOWER CURRENT

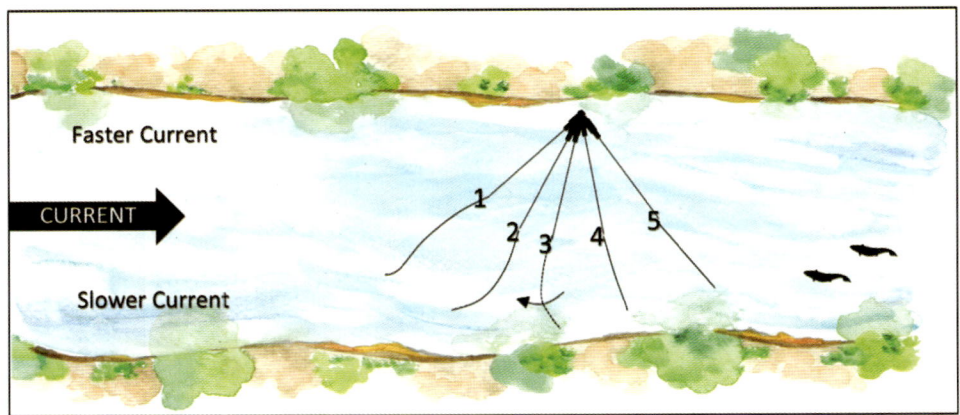

STACK MEND

As previously mentioned, mending is the process of controlling your fly line to avoid creating drag on your fly. Drag is mainly caused when your fly line and fly travel at different speeds because of different currents. For example, the current on the surface where your floating line is drifting is faster than the current below the surface where your wet fly is drifting so the current pulls your fly line downstream faster than your fly causing drag. Trout have a keen ability to know when you fly is not acting like the real insects, they are used to seeing drift down stream and will refuse to strike. Another example is when you cast across two different currents and your fly line and fly are pulled downstream at 2 different speeds. Putting line slack on the water, mending (covered later in this book), and controlling your line are all ways to eliminate drag. Another method is to use a Stack Mend cast that puts an extra amount of line onto the water at the conclusion of your forward cast.

STEPS:

1. Be cautious when you enter the water and avoid kicking up debris that may travel downstream and frighten fish. Make your regular cast upstream (1) and follow your fly and line as it travels downstream.
2. If a belly forms in your line, mend to your right to remove it (2). Strip out some extra line and hold it in your line hand to keep it from floating downstream.
3. When your fly, leader and line start to float downstream past you,

start to feed the extra line out onto the water either by slightly shaking the tip of your rod side-to-side to release line out onto the water or by throwing mini roll casts (3). Don't shake the tip in too wide of an arc or make too big of roll casts and alter the natural drift of your fly. Try and get the extra line to land in front of your position so it travels in the same path as the line that is already on the water. Only cast out 1 or 2 feet of extra slack at a time so you don't release too much slack in case you get a strike. Too much slack will make it much harder to set the hook. Continue your presentation toward your target (4).

READING THE WATER

Presenting Your Fly

BEFORE YOU FISH

The term "Reading the Water" refers to your ability to identify the areas of the river that have the best potential to hold fish (these are called lies), knowing how the current is flowing, and knowing what insects are present and what flies to use to match them. I always take some time when I arrive at a new fishing spot to walk up and down the banks, observe, and identify the lies where I think fish will be, determine if I see fish feeding, and look at the currents. If possible, find a high spot that looks down on the river or stream where you can see a good portion of the water. I also try and visit a river when the water level is lower because it is easier to identify the prime lies like rocks or logs that will be covered by the water when the levels rise. Sketch out some diagrams of these areas so that you can find them again each time you return. I suggest visiting your favorite fishing spot during each season because this will help you identify lies that may not be visible to you last time you were there. Drawing a map of where these objects are also helps. The sketch below is from one of my notebooks.

I also try and answer a few important questions before I start fishing.

- Where is the main current obstructed (slowed down) enough to offer fish protection from the current, shelter from predators, and/or a consistent delivery of food?
- Will I have to cast across multiple currents based on where I plan to stand?
- Are there any visible signs of fish present and if yes, what clues does it offer me about how they are feeding and at what depth?
- Are there any insects present that will help me identify what fly to use?

READING THE WATER

TROUT BEHAVIOR

Purchasing the right gear and learning to use it correctly is only part of the epic battle that has played out between fly fisher and fish for hundreds of years. It is also important to understand how trout (and other fish) behave and to be able to identify the areas of water that have the best potential to hold fish (known as prime lies) and then use that knowledge to improve your chances to catch fish.

Trout behavior changes in relation to the weather and water temperature conditions. Trout like cooler water because there are higher levels of oxygen present, and they have more energy. The levels of oxygen decrease and so does the activity of trout as water temperatures increase. Forty-eight to fifty-eight° Fahrenheit is the optimal water temperature for catching trout because they are most active. Combine that water temperature with an insect hatch and you will have a very exciting day of fishing. There are also times in late June, July and August when the water temperature is simply too hot to fish (especially if you catch and release you increase the chance that the trout will not survive). The illustration below shows you the temperature range for trout and for some of the common insect hatches.

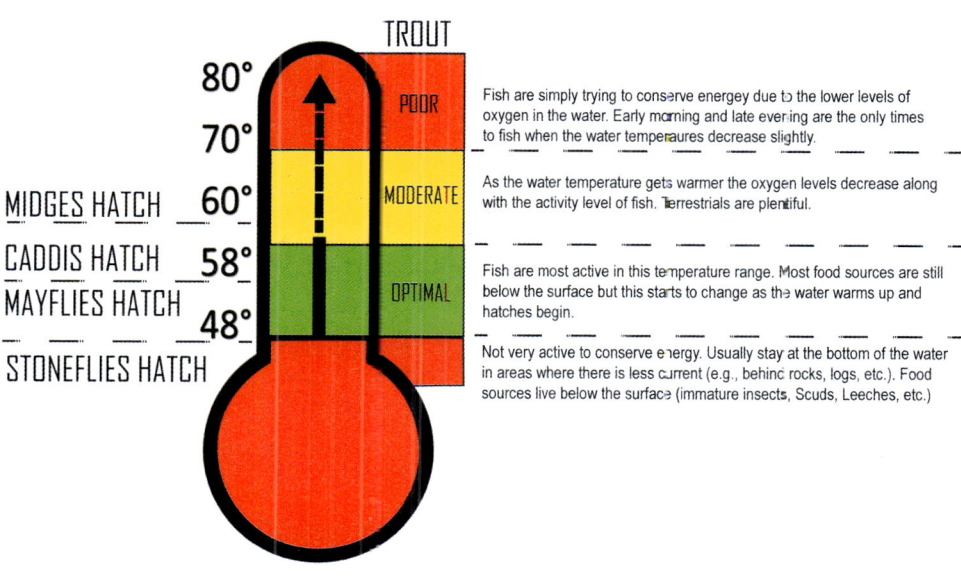

TROUT SENSES

Trout live to eat, not get eaten, reproduce, and not get caught by you. Learning about the anatomy of a trout will help you be a better fly fisher. Trout do not have good binocular vision (the ability for both eyes to see the same object at the same time). The illustration below should help you understand more about a trout's senses.

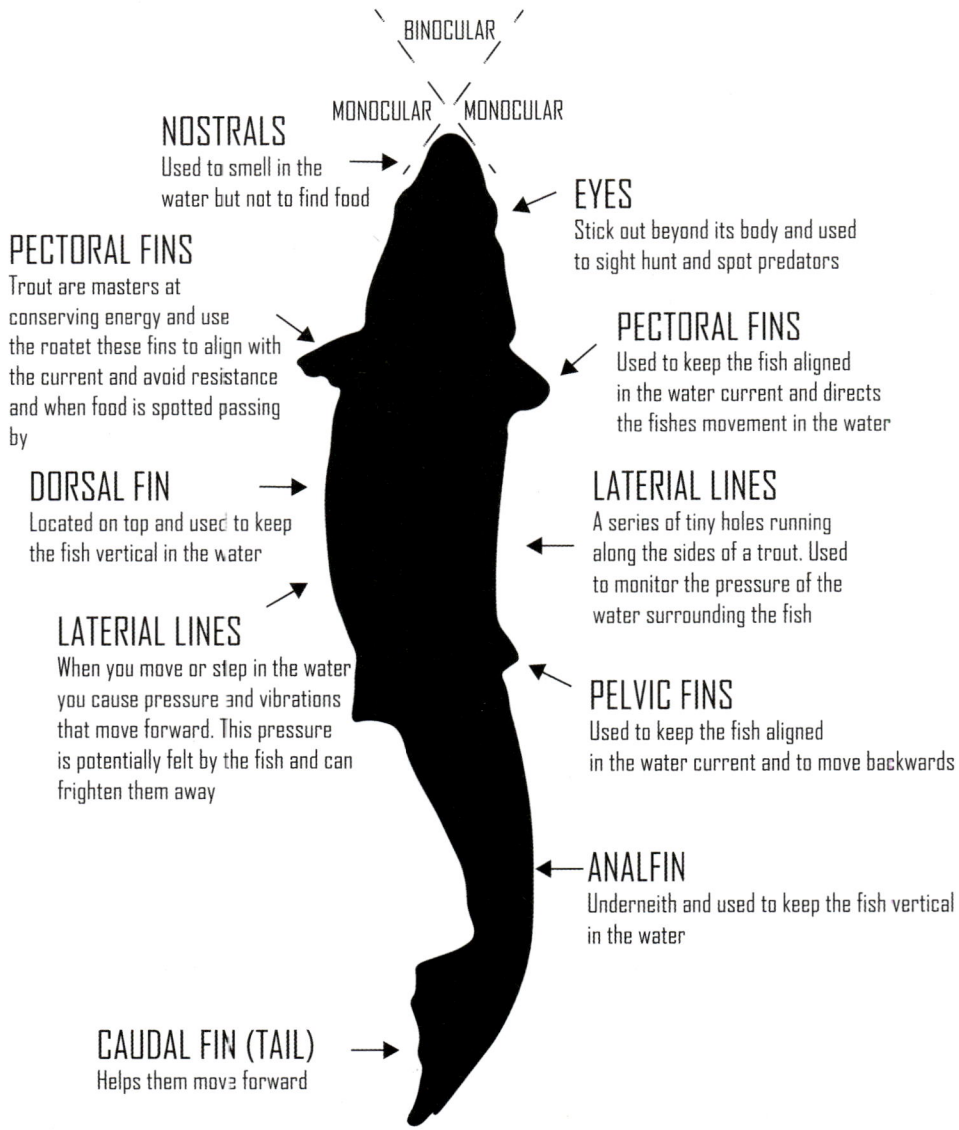

NOSTRALS
Used to smell in the water but not to find food

PECTORAL FINS
Trout are masters at conserving energy and use the roatet these fins to align with the current and avoid resistance and when food is spotted passing by

DORSAL FIN
Located on top and used to keep the fish vertical in the water

LATERIAL LINES
When you move or step in the water you cause pressure and vibrations that move forward. This pressure is potentially felt by the fish and can frighten them away

CAUDAL FIN (TAIL)
Helps them move forward

EYES
Stick out beyond its body and used to sight hunt and spot predators

PECTORAL FINS
Used to keep the fish aligned in the water current and directs the fishes movement in the water

LATERIAL LINES
A series of tiny holes running along the sides of a trout. Used to monitor the pressure of the water surrounding the fish

PELVIC FINS
Used to keep the fish aligned in the water current and to move backwards

ANALFIN
Underneith and used to keep the fish vertical in the water

CONE OF VISION

Trout rely heavily on their senses, especially on what they can see. They use their eyes to spot food, predators, and move around obstacles in the water. Research tells us that most of the light is reflected off the water, so a trout's eyes are designed to function in low light. A trout's eye location also helps them to see all around and not just in front of them. Trout have very good peripheral vision which helps them to spot food and predators easily. Trout are not reliant on color, so it is more important that your fly act as naturally as possible based on the insect you are trying to imitate, as opposed to matching the insects color.

Depth plays a big role in what trout can see. Research tells us that a trout can see about 2 times the depth the fish is swimming (refer to the first illustration below). The second illustration shows you how best to approach a trout based on their cone of vision.

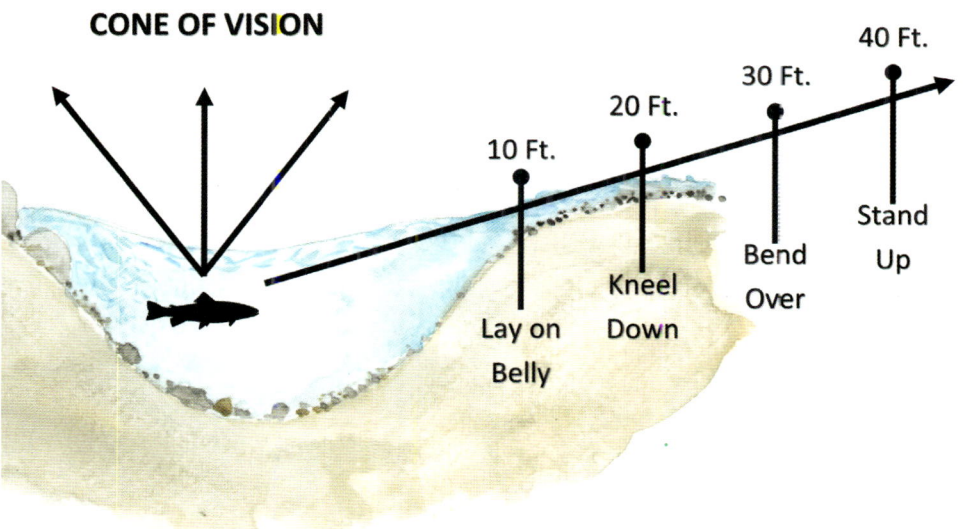

see additional image on page 96

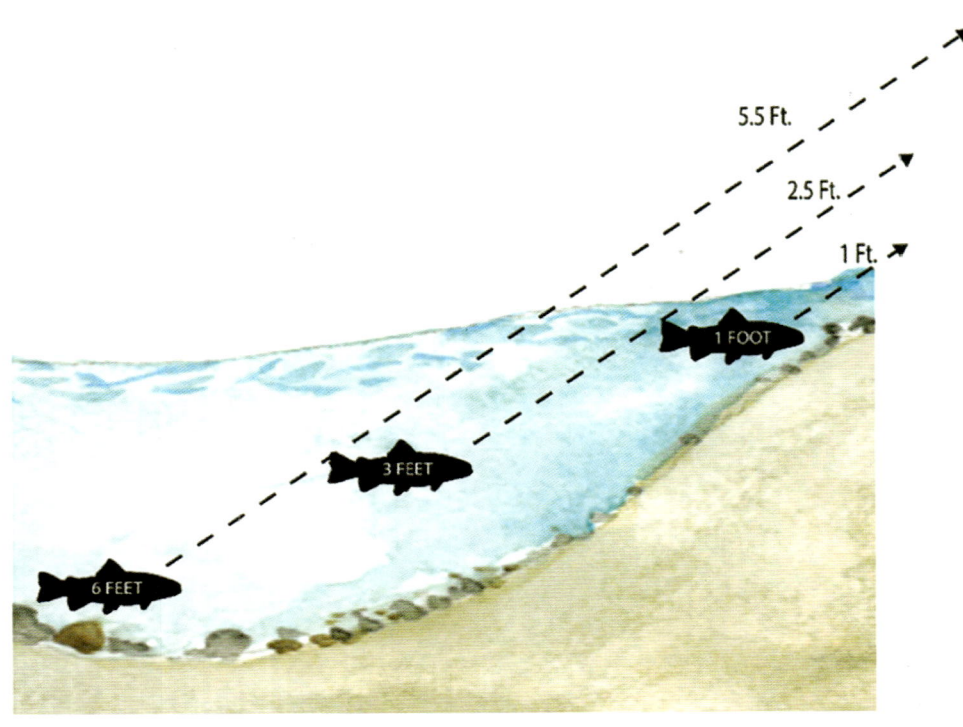

READING THE WATER

RIVER SECTIONS

The Riffle, Run and Pool are the 3 major sections of a river. These sections repeat over the length of a river. Each section has its own unique characteristics and lies where fish hide that are important for fly fishers to learn about to improve your chances to find and catch fish.

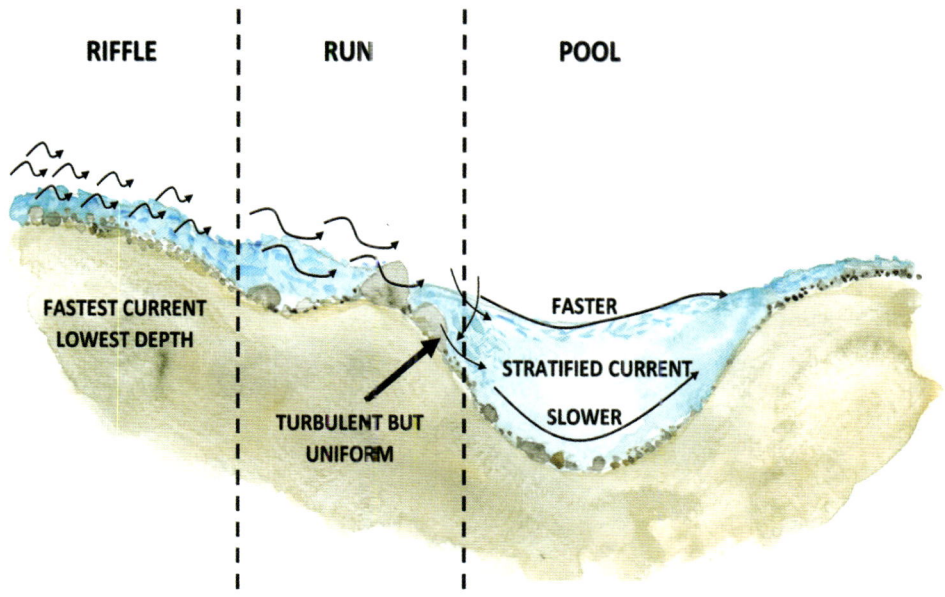

THE RIFFLE

A riffle is the fastest and most turbulent section of a river caused by a shallow depth and rocky bottom. Riffles are important to the health of a river due to the oxygen it provides that keeps the river and fish healthy. The riffle is usually not an area where many fish will hold for long periods of time because this area does not offer a lot of protection from the fast current or from overhead predators due to the shallow depth. Fish will hide behind larger rocks or other submerged or semi-submerged objects in the water that protect them from the faster current and dart in and out of the faster current just long enough to eat what is passing by and then swim back to a more protective spot behind a rock or log that protects them from a fast current. The riffle is a good habitat for insects because of the lack of fish and the abundance of oxygen. Don't let the shallow depth fool you. The current is still stratified (faster on the surface and slower on the bottom) with the potential to cause drag.

The fast current means that you will have to cast your fly far enough upstream of your target to give yourself time to eliminate drag if it occurs. The turbulence also means that you may have to use a more buoyant dry fly to keep it afloat on the surface or use a lightly weighted wet fly to keep it from dragging on the bottom or getting stuck. Look for fish holding behind semi and/or submerged objects where the depth may be deeper and the current slower. The area behind these objects is known as an eddy and is a prime lie (covered later in this book).

To fish a riffle, I suggest positioning yourself downstream or adjacent to the riffle and then use a casting grid (covered later in this book) to divide the riffle into partitions a foot or two wide. Try and find any rocks or objects submerged or semi-submerged in the water and drift your fly past them. This is an area, sometimes referred to as a pocket or eddy (covered later in this book. This is an area where the fish will hold because the speed of the current is reduced by the object.

THE RUN

A Run is the second faster section of a river. It is a less turbulent area of the river because the depth is deeper and the bottom usually smoother. Even if rocks are present, they cause less turbulence because the water is deeper. Deeper water provides more protection for fish from predators and faster current.

It is sometimes easier to identify potential lies and spot fish in the river from a higher vantage point (like a boulder or high spot on the bank) where you can look down on a section of the river. Darker areas of the river will usually be the deeper sections.

Areas known as "Pocket Water" or "An Eddy" are some of the best places to find fish. Pocket water is the spot where the faster current is slowed down when it is forced against semi and/or submerged objects (rocks, boulders, trees, etc.) and the current is slowed down and forced to move around the object at a slower speed. Fish will hold in these "pockets" because they use less energy and wait for their next meal to be delivered to them by the current or dart in and out of the faster current to eat an insect (or hopefully your fly) as it passes by. The targets on the illustration on page 99 show potential Pocket Water and Eddy's.

READING THE WATER

RIVER SECTIONS | 107

THE POOL

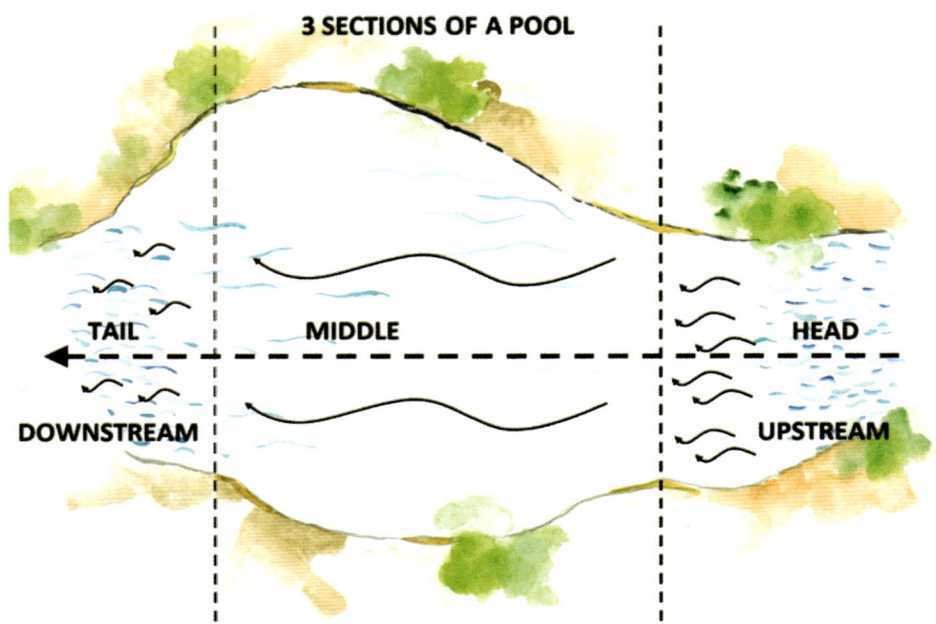

The run spills into the pool which is the deepest and calmest section of a river. A pool can be divided into 3 basic sections:

1. The Head – This is where the faster and more turbulent current from the run spills in and mixes with the slower current and deeper depth of the pool. This is good place to find fish because they feed on the food that gets trapped where the two currents meet.

2. The Middle – This is usually the deepest section of the pool and provides the most protection for fish from predators and from faster currents. It is also a place that delivers fish a good deal of food. This is usually where the largest fish will hold. The current begins to stratify in the middle of the pool and tends to be faster on the surface than at the bottom. You will need to sink your wet fly down deeper in this section unless fish are feeding on or near the surface.

3. The Tail – At the rear of the pool the depth begins to decrease, and the current starts to speed up again with the transition to the next riffle. Fish holding in the middle and tail of a pool will also rise to sip insects at the surface of the pool if they are available.

The darker colored areas of the pool are the deepest so make sure to calculate how far down you need to sink your wet fly in relation to where you believe the fish are holding. I suggest starting at the head of the pool and work your way toward the tail. One of my favorite spots to fish is standing behind a large bolder in the middle of a run. I let my fly drift down the run and into the pool. I usually get a strike as my fly drifts into the head of the pool.

PRIME LIES

A prime lie is an area of a river or stream where fish will potentially be present. Trout are relatively lazy (like me) and usually do not want to exert any more energy than is necessary to eat a nutritious and satisfying meal. Trout need to balance the amount of energy they expel swimming against the current, chasing food, and avoiding predators, against the amount of energy they gain from the nutrients in the food they eat. Trout will usually wait in a prime lie and dart in and out of a faster current to eat and then return to where it feels protected. The fish may also stay in the prime lie because insects are drifting close enough to it that it doesn't have to expel a lot of energy to eat.

Prime lies can usually be found on the sides of the main current (the main current of a river or stream can be identified by locating the trail of debris or foam floating down the river or stream).

Prime lies have the following factors in common:

1. **Protection from Predators:** Fish will hold in areas of a river or stream where they feel protected from overhead predators like birds and humans. Deeper depths are usually found in pools but other areas behind rocks, trees, under/overhanging bushes or banks, or in submerged tree roots also provide protection. A frightened fish will not feed and not feel threatened before the fish will start to feed and/or be interested in your fly.

2. **Consistent Delivery of Food:** Fish will wait on the sides of the main current in areas of a river where the current is slower and wait for food to be delivered to them at a slower pace.

3. **Shelter from Fast Current:** Fish, especially trout, will conserve their energy and not waste it chasing food or holding in faster currents. Fish will find lies where the faster main current is slowed down like areas behind large rocks, in pools, behind fallen trees, etc. These lies give provide the fish with the option of darting in and out of the main current to feed.

4. **Adequate Oxygen:** Fish need an adequate supply of oxygen in the water to remain active and survive. Turbulent water has the most oxygen but must also be deep enough and offer enough places with shelter from the fast current for fish to remain in these areas. Keep in mind that the faster current is usually caused by a shallow river or stream with a rough bottom. Rivers and streams without an adequate supply of oxygen become stagnant and are not as healthy as a river or stream with a good flow of water and may not be able to sustain fish.

5. **Water Temperature:** Fish are more active in moderate water temperatures. When the water temperature is too hot or too cold, fish become inactive to conserve energy and survive. Water temperature can be measured by purchasing a special thermometer available in most fly or sporting goods stores. The water temperature will usually dictate how successful you will be in catching fish. Side streams usually deliver colder water into the main part of a river and lowers the water temperature in that spot making it a prime lie in warmer weather.

READING THE WATER

The diagram below illustrates the type of prime lies to look for on a river or stream. Each lie will be explored in more detail on the pages that follow.

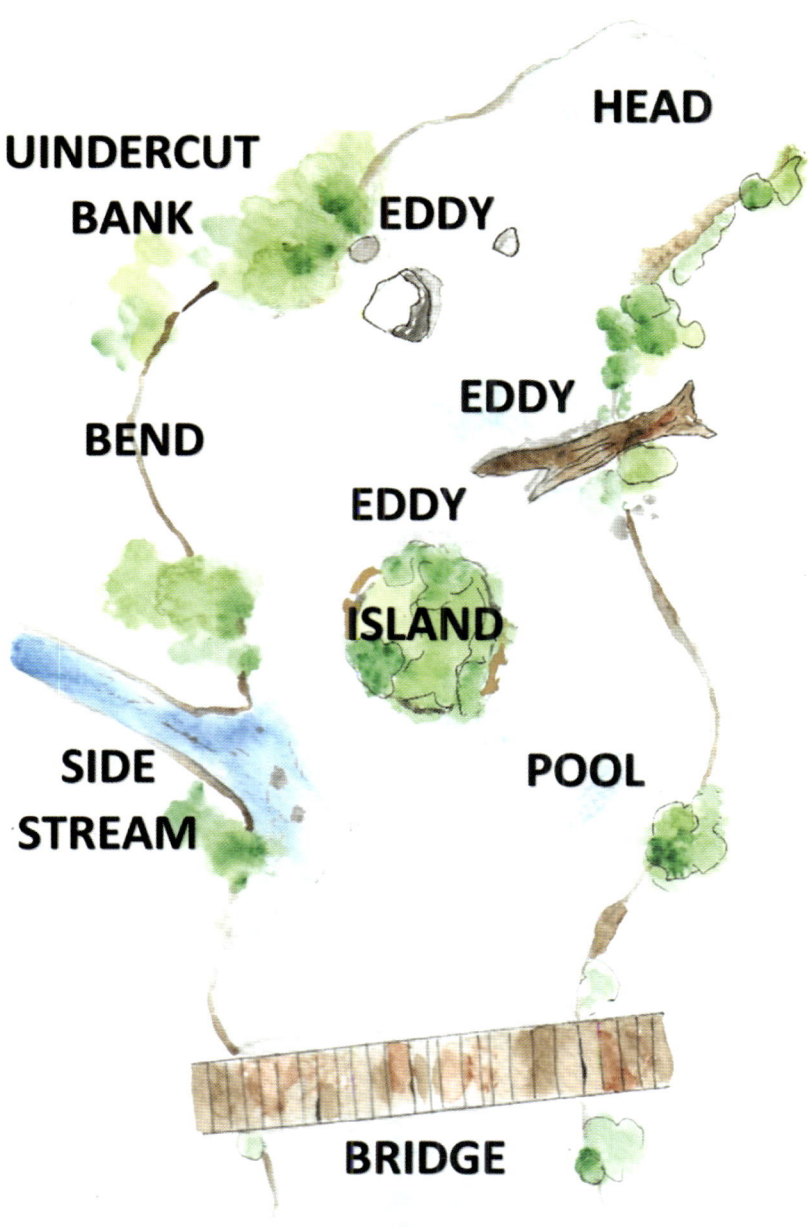

PRIME LIES | 111

THE EDDY

An eddy is the area at the rear of a submerged or semi-submerged object (e.g., large rock, log, etc.). that the current cannot move. The faster current is slowed down when it pushes into the immoveable object and forces the faster current around the sides of the object while slowing down the current in the space directly behind the object in the water. This makes the Eddy a prime lie because food (or your fly imitating food) drifts down in the current past the object in the water and the fish can quickly swim into the faster current and grab its next meal (or your fly) and then back into the prime lie where the current is slower.

The area just past the eddy where the current begins to regain speed (known as the "Lee Pocket) is also an area where fish may hold. Also look for fish holding in the front of the object or on the sides if the current is slow enough.

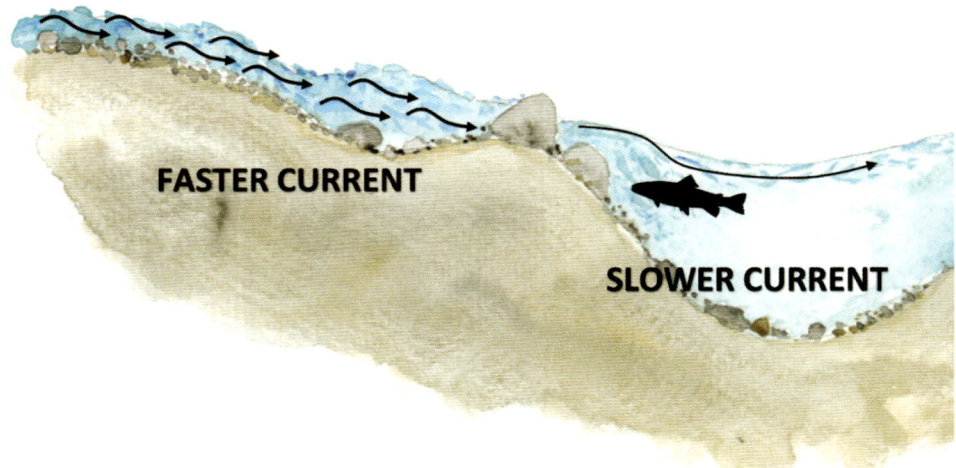

READING THE WATER

This is where fish will wait because the current is not as strong. Fish will hold here and dart in and out of the faster current carrying food.

Faster current diverted around the rock

PRESENTATION TO AN EDDY

I usually approach an eddy upstream and wade carefully into the water to avoid frightening the fish with any debris that I might kick. Try and cast your fly far enough upstream of the eddy to give yourself time to move your fly into position and eliminate any errors like drag (1). You want your fly to drift close to the submerged object, pass it by, and encourage any fish hiding in the eddy to strike. In the illustration below you are casting downstream and across the river. Mend if needed to eliminate drag and reposition your fly if needed. Drift your fly down toward the front of the eddy first (2) and then down the side closest to you (this may take a few casts). I have found that this is usually where fish will strike (4). Continue to drift your fly downstream past the eddy where fish will also hold and where the current begins to pick up speed (5). This area is known as the "Lee Pocket." Make stack mends to add slack in your line and extend your presentation if you like to continue the drift.

Reposition yourself if you like and try the other side of the eddy if possible. If you look at the illustration below, you could cross to the opposite side of the river and make a downstream presentation to the eddy from the water or try presenting your fly while standing on the bank.

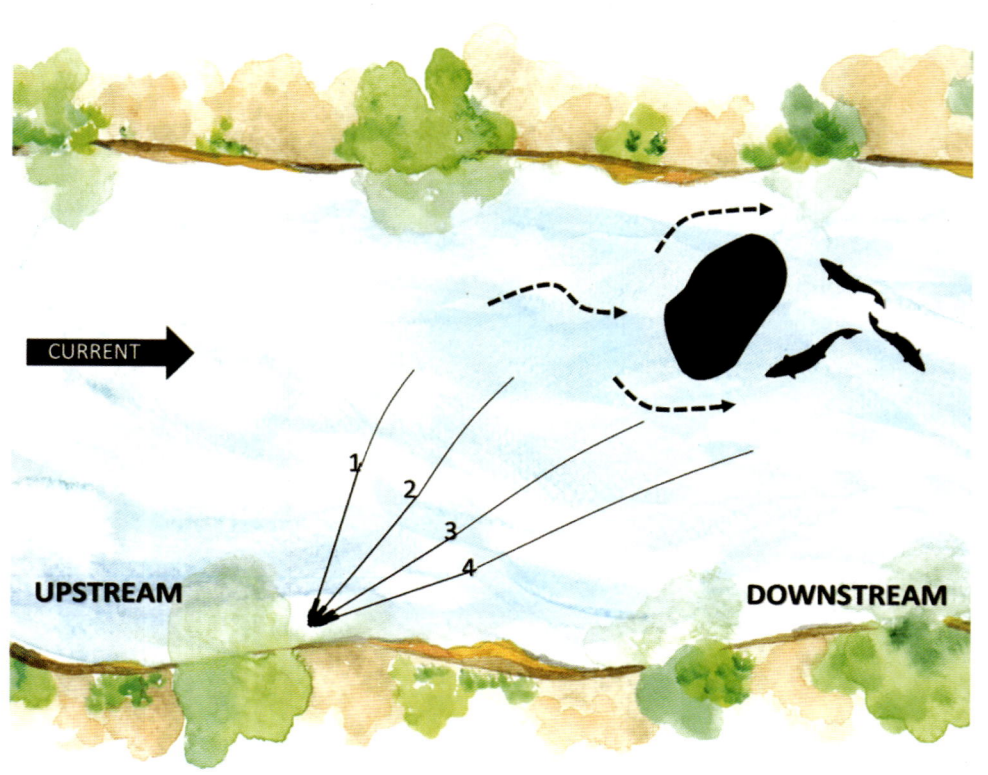

READING THE WATER

THE ISLAND

Approach the presentation to an island similar to how you present to an eddy. An island is a prime lie because it provides fish with the same type of shelter as an Eddy. There is the added potential for insects, frogs, or mice to jump off of the island into the water, fall off a tree or bush, or get blown into the water by the wind.

PRESENTATION TO AN ISLAND

Choose which side of the island that you plan to fish first. Approach the island upstream and avoid frightening fish with any debris that you might kick up while wading into the water that will drift downstream. Cast your fly far enough upstream of the island to give yourself time to get your fly into position and correct any errors. You can also make a downstream cast or cast downstream and across. In the illustration below I show a downstream cast (1). Be ready to add slack into your line quickly if you cast directly downstream because the current will quickly remove any slack in your line. If you cast across, or downstream and across, be ready to mend if needed and/or add slack if needed (2). Let your fly drift past the island and past the eddy at the rear of the island where fish may hold. Work the other side of the island next if possible. If you are using a popper or grasshopper imitation fly, try casting across onto the island and then pulling your fly off the bank into the water to simulate an amphibian jumping off into the water.

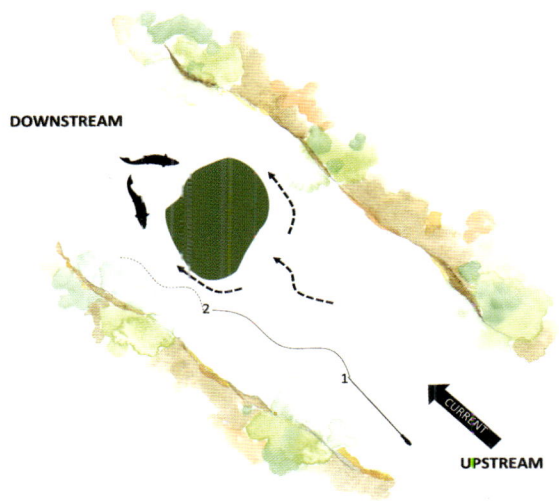

see additional image on page 110

UNDERCUT BANKS

An undercut bank is usually found on the curve of a river or stream that has severe bends. Undercut banks are formed when the current forces itself against the bank and friction and debris erode the loose soil underneath the bank and cuts into the underside of the bank. This is a prime lie because fish can hide under the overhang of the bank or under bushes or grass hanging over the bank. The overhang also provides fish with shade, cooler water temperatures, and protection from overhead predators. The current that travels into and close to the back delivers food to fish making it a great place for fish to hold. Land-based insects like grasshoppers, ants, etc. also have the potential to get knocked into the water by the wind for fish to eat.

PRESENTATION TO AN UNDERCUT BANK

Enter the water upstream of the target area and be cautious not to kick up wading debris that may travel downstream and frighten the fish. Cast far enough upstream and across to the bank to give yourself time to move your fly into position and correct any errors by mending or adding slack (1 & 2). Add slack as needed and get your fly to drift in front of or slightly underneath the undercut bank (3). You can also move far enough upstream of the bank and use a downstream cast. Once you complete that presentation you can recast and try and get your fly further under the bank if possible.

If you are using a hopper or other fly that imitates a terrestrial or mouse, try casting across onto the bank and pull your fly off quickly into the water to imitate a terrestrial that has been blown into the water by the wind or a frog hopping off the bank into the water. Make sure and land your fly on the upstream side of the weeds so that it drifts under the bank when you pull it off into the water. If you leave your fly on the bank too long your line will start to drift downstream faster than your fly and cause drag (see image of page 109).

READING THE WATER

SIDE STREAMS

Side streams are smaller streams that feed colder water into the main body of a river. Side streams are prime lies because food gets trapped, the water temperature is cooler, and the depth can often be deeper where the current of the side stream and current of the main river mix together.

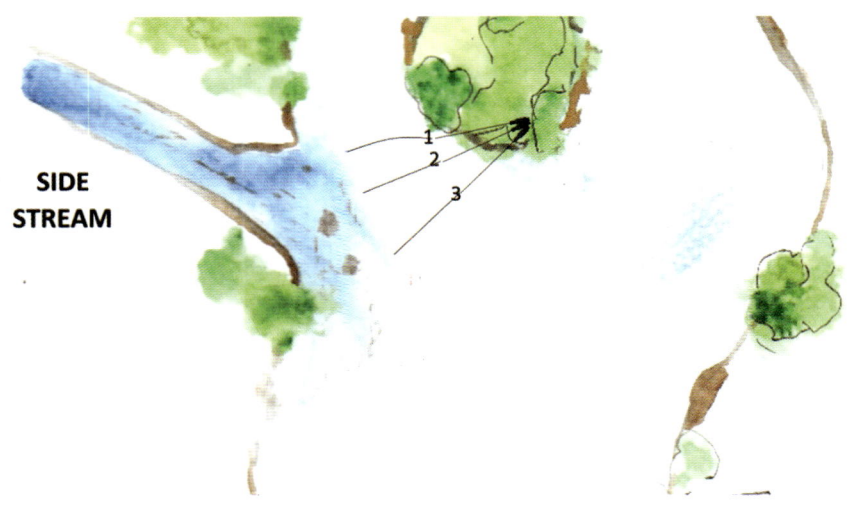

PRESENTATION TO A SIDE STREAM

Enter the water and be careful to avoid casting over the fish or frightening them with wading debris that you may kick up. Make your cast across and upstream (1) far enough ahead of the side stream so that you have time to correct any issues before your fly reaches the side stream and your target area (2). Mend if necessary. Follow your line and fly with your rod and let your fly drift through the area where the two currents meet (3). If there is an island or boulder to stand on use that. You can also position yourself upstream of the side stream and make a downstream cast or stand on the bank upstream of the side stream and cast from that position. Below I show a presentation from the bank of an island across to the side stream.

BENDS

A bend in the river usually offer fish protection from the faster current and provide a consistent delivery and supply of food as it passes by their spot. Fish will usually hold on to the side of the bend where the current is slowest and wait for food to drift by or dart in and out of the faster current to grab a snack.

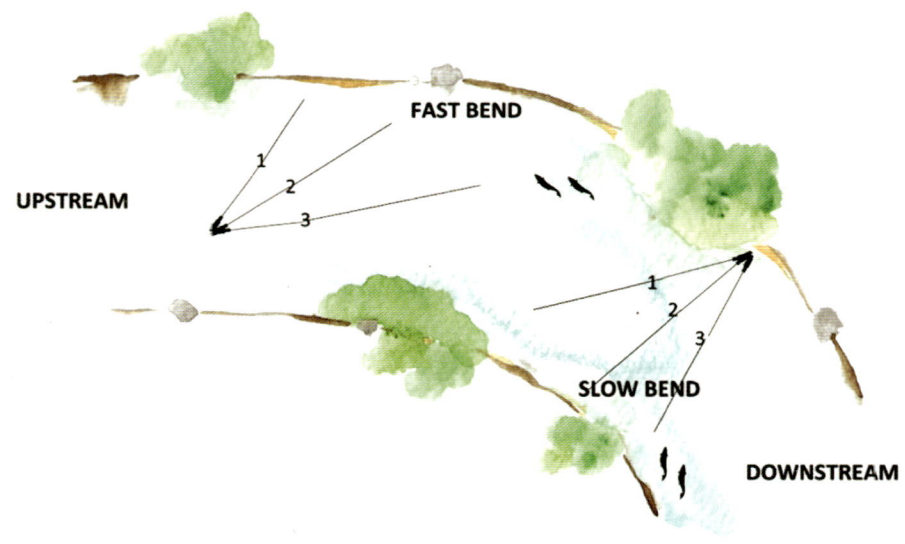

READING THE WATER

PRESENTATION TO A BEND

I usually enter the water upstream of the bend. Be careful not to kick up any debris when you enter the water that can drift downstream and frighten fish. Cast slightly upstream and across of the bend to give yourself time to correct any errors (1). Follow the drift of your line with your rod tip toward your target (2). Use stack mends if necessary to add slack into the presentation and animate your fly as needed. Follow your fly with the tip of your rod toward your target and avoid drag (3).

OTHER LIES

Flats: A flat is a shallow, slow moving area of a river or stream where weeds usually grow to the top of the surface of the water. The current passes over the tops of the weeds and the weeds act like a net often catching insects and other food that drifts downstream. Flats are also good habitats for insects because the current is slower and there are a lot of places to hide and be protected from fish. Keep in mind that wet flies may get snagged in the weeds so its sometimes best to use a buoyant dry fly that can easily drift on the surface of the water over the top of the flat enticing fish below to strike. Some flies, like peppers, can be tied with weed guards (a thin piece of monofilament) that prevents them from getting tangled up in weeded areas.

Bridges: Bridges provide protection for fish from overhead predators and shade that keeps the water temperature cooler under the bridge in the summer months. Fish will hold under bridges in the shadows along the edges or along the pilings of the bridge. Try casting across and letting your fly drift downstream under the bridge. Throw stack mends to lengthen your drift after it passes under the bridge.

Submerged Tree Roots: The roots of trees growing on the edge of the bank often protrude into the water. These roots provide fish with protection from overhead predators, shelter from the faster current, and are a natural trap for drifting food. Fish will forage among tree roots searching for food. Try drifting your fly in front of or over the roots to avoid getting your fly snagged in the roots.

RISE FORMS

To strike or not to strike....that is the fish question. Fish usually spend time observing your fly before deciding to take or refuse it. Below is an illustration of one way a fish will rise to inspect your fly.

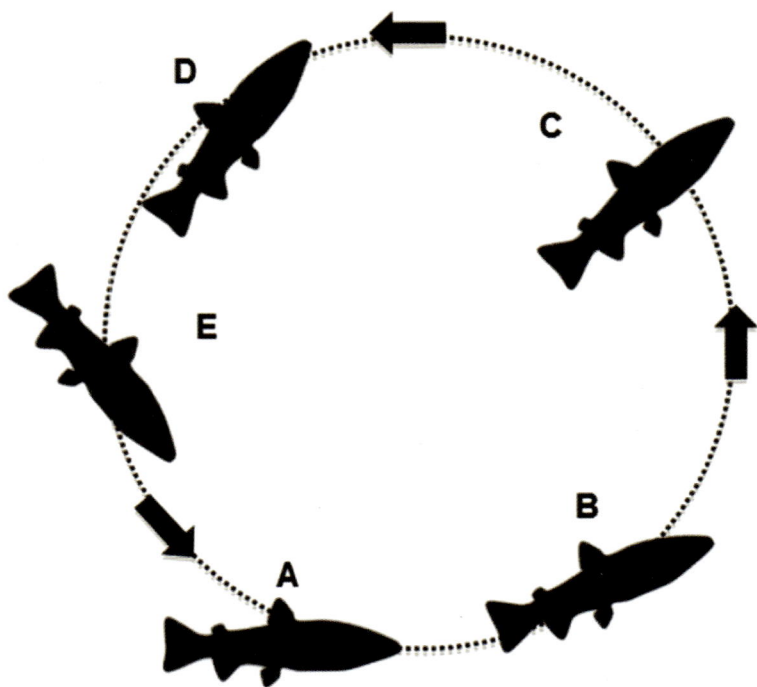

A.   The fish lies in wait for food
B.   The fish sees the fly and begins to rise to inspect it
C.   The fish continues to drift and inspect the fly
D.   The fish refuses the fly or takes it
E.   The fish returns to its lie

The fish exerts the most energy between B to E

READING THE WATER

A rise usually occurs downstream of where a fish eats. After it rises, the fish will usually move back upstream and wait for more food to arrive. Rises help you determine where fish are feeding and give you clues as to what they are eating (depending on the time of day, insects that live in the river, temperature, and location of the river), and what fly to use.

Below are the different types of rises and the clues they will give you about what and how fish are eating.

SIMPLE, COMPOUND AND COMPLEX RISES

In each of these rises, the fish lies in wait and starts to rise at it sees a potential food source approaching (1 & 2). It's snout or head breaks the surface (3) as it feeds on the food source on the surface of the water. In a Simple rise, the fish is confident of the food source and does not take long inspecting it before it strikes. In a Compound and Complex rise, the fish takes more time inspecting the food source before deciding if it will strike. The fish returns to where it was holding or continues feeding if more of the same food is present (4).

READING THE WATER

SIP RISE

The fish lies in wait and starts to rise at it sees a potential food source approaching (1 & 2). snout and head usually break the surface of the water. It is feeding on or sipping a food source on the surface of the water (3).

HEAD TO TAIL RISE

The fish lies in wait and starts to rise at it sees a potential food source approaching (1 & 2). The fish feeds on a food source below the surface and its head and then tail is visible at times (3 & 4).

READING THE WATER

TAIL RISE

The fish lies in wait and starts to rise at it sees a potential food source approaching (1 & 2). The fish is feeding on a food source in the middle or bottom position of the water and its tail is sometimes visible.

BULGE RISE

The fish is feeding on a food source in the insects in the surface film of the water. These are most likely insects getting ready to mature and fly out of the water or are already dead.

RISE FORMS | 125

PRESENTATIONS

The term "presentation" refers to many things. It incorporates the strategies and techniques you use to entice a fish to strike at your imitation fly, your read of the water, fly selection, water and weather conditions, and more. No matter how expensive your gear is you will not catch fish if you don't learn to present your fly effectively in different ways.

You would not want to hire a plumber who only uses a blow torch to fix every plumbing issue like a clogged sink. You would expect the plumber to have an array of "practiced" experiences and different tools to choose from to fix the issue at hand. I encourage you to approach fly fishing in the same way and experiment with different presentation strategies and to create your own variations to match the situations you face each time your fish. Just because a presentation is referred to as a "wet fly swing" doesn't mean that it will not work in some other way. The more you experiment, the more you will find out what does and does not work and ultimately, catch more fish. Experimenting and trying various techniques is what I love most about fly fishing. Keep notes as you experiment.

Your goal is to figure out how to get the fish to bite. Answering the questions below is a good first step to help you do just that.

1. Will my fly and fly line travel in different current speeds after I cast?
2. How far ahead of my target will I need to cast to give myself time to correct issues?
3. Will I need to use extra weight to sink my fly to the depth where fish are eating?
4. Does my fly and my presentation imitate the food fish are eating?
5. Have I been as stealthy as possible wading in the water?
6. Can I cast from downstream of my target to avoid scaring fish with debris I may loosen?
7. Can I make my presentation from the land so I don't have to wade?
8. Can I see any fish behaviors that give me clues to what and how they are eating?
9. Have I eliminated drag from my presentation so my fly doesn't act unnaturally?
10. Is my tippet long enough so the fish sees my fly first and not my leader or line?
11. Have I frightened the fish by landing my fly too hard on the water?
12. Have I made my wet fly drift at the same depth as the fish?
13. Have I studied the water currents and depth to make sure your presentation is correct?

READING THE WATER

BASIC PRESENTATION

While there are many ways to present your fly, your presentation also depends on your ability to analyze your target area, the current, what fish are eating and the type of fly you are using (wet or dry). Rivers and streams consist of different sections of fast and slow water that is dictated by the depth of the water and the rockiness of the bottom. Consider these factors before you cast:

Distance to your target - Faster water often requires that you cast further upstream ahead of your target to give yourself time to move your fly into position, sink your fly to the desired depth (for wet flies), eliminate drag, animate your fly (if necessary), and get yourself ready to set the hook if a strike occurs. The best position is always the one that gets you closest to the fish without the fish seeing you.

Amount of deception needed - The turbulence of faster water decreases the distance fish can see so you need to present your fly closer to the fish to entice a strike while slower currents create usually increase the distance a fish will be able to see. Slower water requires more stealth, softer casts without splashes, use more natural looking flies, and the use of longer tippet so the fly reaches the fish well ahead of your leader and line.

Use of weight - Faster water means that your wet fly will need to sink quicker, and you will need to adjust the distance your cast ahead of your target to give yourself time to adjust your presentation.

There are 5 basic ways to present your fly (and lots of variations), (1) Upstream; (2) Upstream and Across; (3) Across; (4) Downstream and Across; and (5) Downstream.

Each of these presentations are covered in detail on the next few pages and can be varied and used with dry and wet flies. Once you learn them, you can begin to make variations to suit your fly fishing situation.

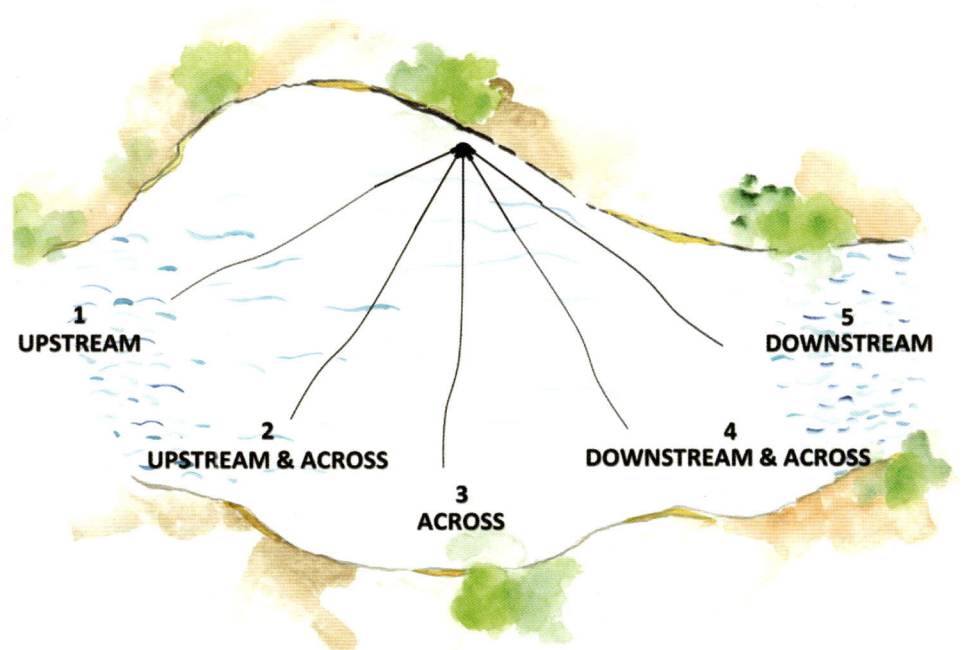

STRATEGIES

USING WEIGHT

Weight is used to sink your wet fly to a specific depth where fish are feeding or holding. Some ways weight can be added include:

Split Shot - Small, different size weights that are crimped onto the leader with pliers or forceps.

Twist-on/Pinch-on - Small thin strips that are twisted or pinched on the leader.

Tied on - Weight can be added to a fly when it is tied either by wrapping it around the shank of the hook under the body material or by adding a metal bead or cone head to the fly.

READING THE WATER

Weight makes your cast more difficult so you may need to use a more open casting loop to avoid tangles, slow down your casting stroke, not use false casts, and/or aim your forward cast above your eye level.

The amount of weight you add really depends on the depth where you want your fly to drift, the speed of the current and how fast or slow it allows your fly to sink, the type of fly you are using and/or the buoyancy of your fly.

(The size of the weight in the illustration below is exaggerated for visual effect)

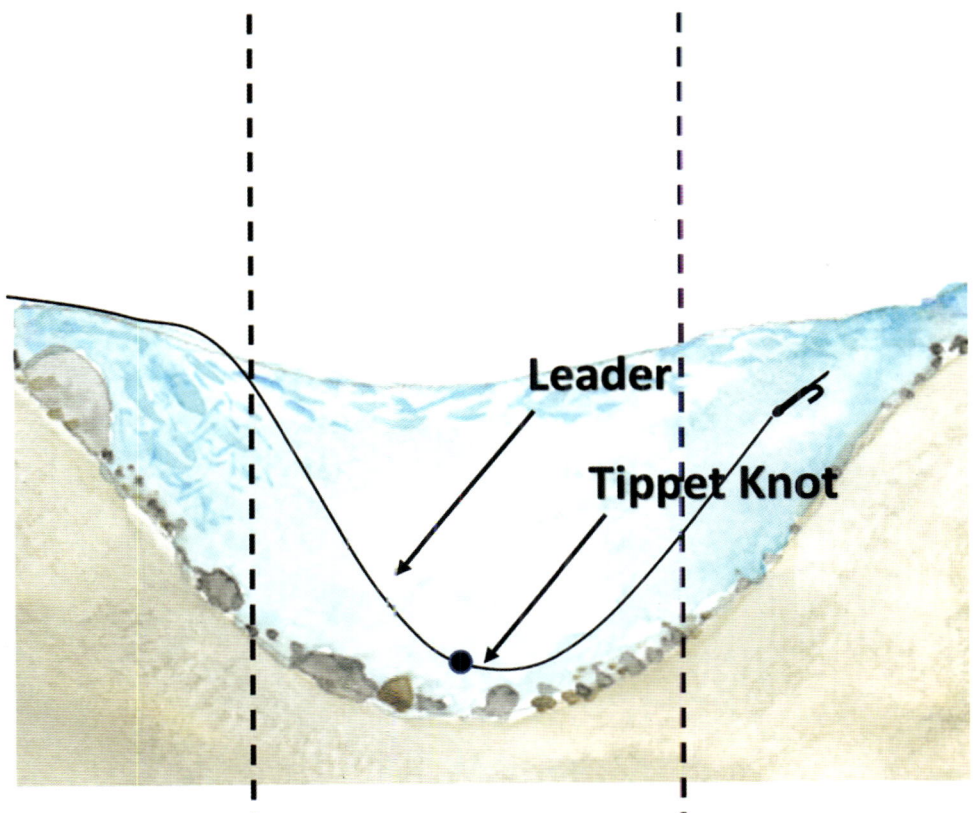

STRATEGIES

STRIKE INDICATORS

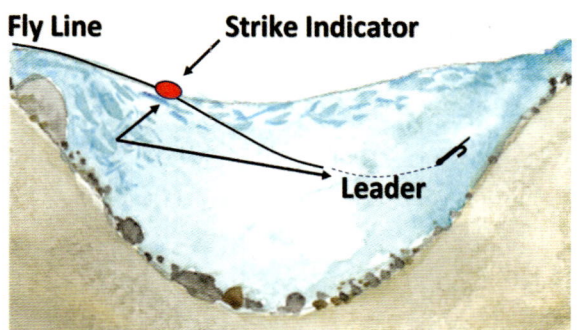

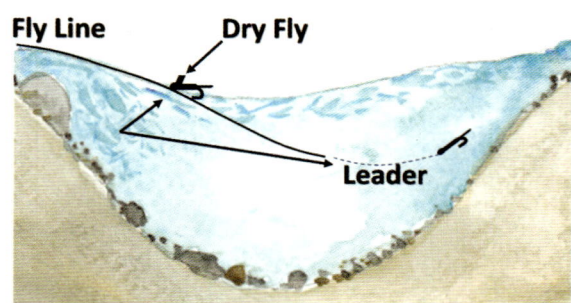

The strike indicator is a mini version of the bobber/bobbin you might have used spin casting. Indicators help you detect strikes when you are unable to see your wet fly that is drifting beneath the surface of the water. Indicators are made from a variety of materials (e.g., yarn, cork, foam, putty, stick-on material, etc.) and are attached on your leader. They are made in bright colors that makes they easy to see on the surface of the water for long distances.

Indicators can also be used as a depth regulator to make your flies float at specific depths below the surface of the water. Some fly fishers refuse to use an indicator because the splash and sight of the indicator drifting on the current may potentially scare fish. Try and keep your indicator and fly in the same current lane to avoid drag from occurring.

The distance that you set your strike indicator from your fly will vary in relation to your fishing situation. In general, the indicator should be set 1.5 - 2 times the depth of the water. This means that the fly is approximately the same distance from the indicator as it is to the surface of the water.

READING THE WATER

A buoyant dry fly can also be used as a strike indicator when it is tied to your wet fly that travels beneath the surface in a multiple fly rig. This doubles your chances to catch a because the fish can strike at either.

CASTING GRID

A casting grid is an imaginary grid that you can use to systematically divide up a smaller section of water to search for fish when none are visible. You work each part of the grid before moving onto the next section. Before you start casting, can you see any visible signs of fish present? If yes, what does it tell you about how and what they are eating (see Rise Forms later in this book)

Picture the grid in your mind for the area of the water you are going to target. Begin by casting upstream to the target area closest to your position (1). This avoids you having to cast over any fish that are holding closest to you and frightening them with your line. Follow your line with your rod tip as it drifts downstream, mend as needed, until your presentation is complete (2, 3, & 4). Repeat your first cast only this time, cast a little further out on the grid and complete your presentation (5, 6, & 7). Repeat the first cast by cast out further and complete your presentation (8, 9, & 10). Repeat this pattern on each section of the grid.

COUNTDOWN SEARCH METHOD

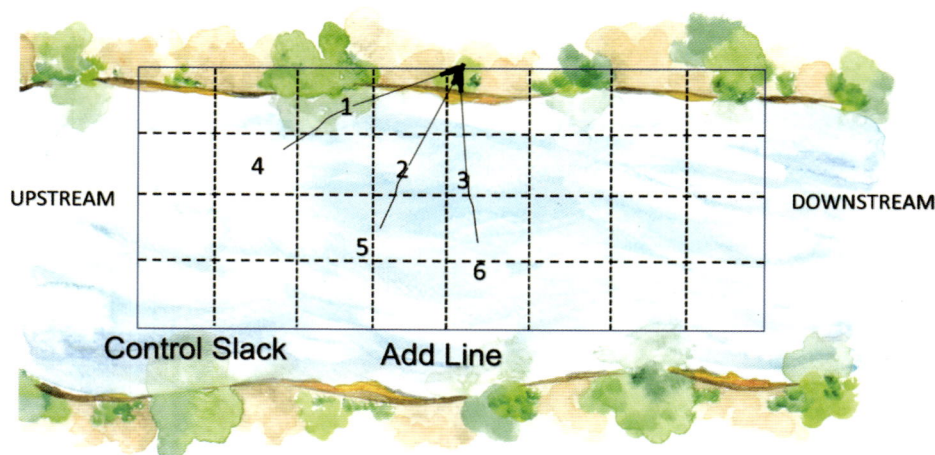

This technique is useful when there are no signs of fish in the water. It is very similar to the casting grid except that you are searching different depths of the water for fish by letting your wet fly sink to various levels of the water when no rises are visible.

Cast upstream to a target area closest to you to avoid casting over the fish closest to your position and frightening them with your line (1). Count to a specific number (e.g., 1, 2, 3) as your wet fly sinks and then retrieve your fly (2). You can add weight if your your wet fly is not sinking fast enough to the depth your desire. Control slack and mend if necessary. Follow your fly and line with your rod tip and continue your presentation (3). You can raise and/or lower your rod tip and control the depth in the water that your fly travels. Repeat the steps above casting out further to the next target area on your grid (4, 5, & 6). Increase or decrease your count and vary the level of your rod and fly.

READING THE WATER

UPSTREAM PRESENTATION

An upstream presentation means that you will need to be prepared to quickly control the return of line back toward you downstream as soon as your fly and line land on the water. There is usually less chance for drag to occur with this type of presentation because your fly and line will be drifting toward you usually in the same current lane. Drag will occur if your fly drifts ahead of the tip of your fly line so make sure to strip in slack as needed. An upstream cast is considered one of the easiest presentations because you will not need to mend or worry about your fly and line traveling in different currents. If the area you are fishing is heavily fished, be aware that the fish may be very aware of overhead fly lines and can scare them off.

MAKING AN UPSTREAM PRESENTATION

Enter the river or stream downstream from your target to avoid frightening the fish with any debris that you will dislodge while wading. Cast upstream and beyond your target and be ready to take in line slack immediately after your cast (1). You want to remove the slack in your line so you can be ready to set the hook should the fish strike. If you are casting a dry fly, make sure to give it a soft landing and avoid your line from making a splash so you have less of a chance to frighten the fish.

UPSTREAM PRESENTATION | 133

Strip/pull in line to control the slack of your line on the water so you are ready to set the hook when the fish strikes (2). You increase your chance of setting the hook when there is less slack in your line.

UPSTREAM & ACROSS PRESENTATION

There is an increased chance for drag to occur with an upstream and across presentation if your fly and line are cast across different types of current (e.g., faster and slower). A faster current has the potential to pull one part of your line downstream quicker than the other part causing drag. Make sure that you analyze the area where you will cast and your fly will travel.

MAKING AN UPSTREAM AND ACROSS PRESENTATION

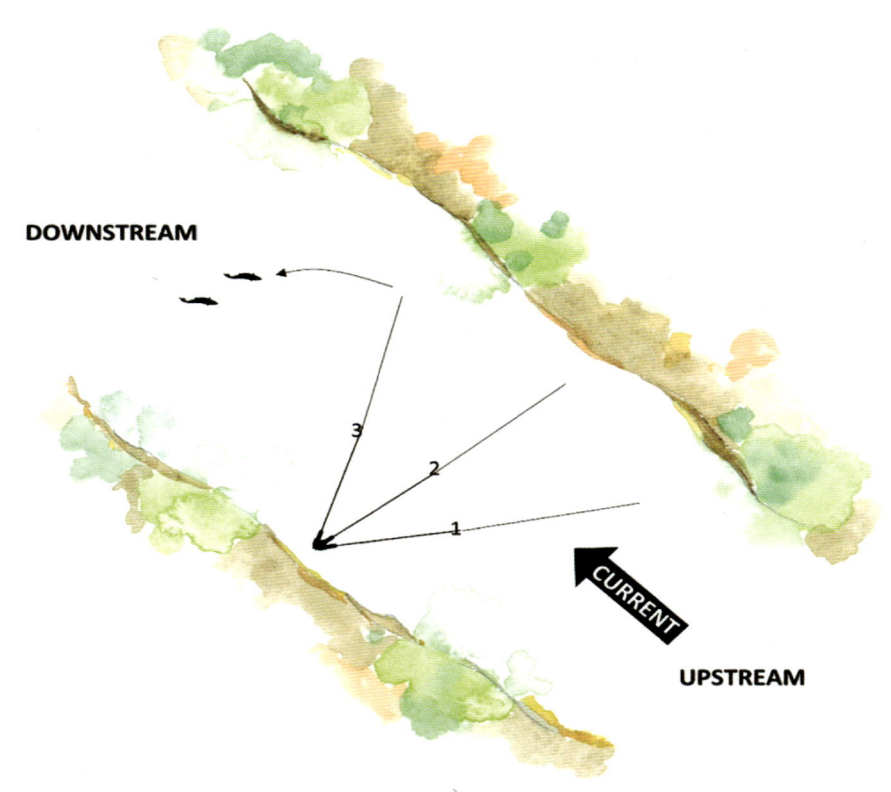

READING THE WATER

Enter the river cautiously to avoid frightening the fish with any debris that you may dislodge when you wade in the water. Keep in mind that a fish has about a 45°angle and may see you. Make a tight cast upstream and across (1). Avoid putting too much slack on the water because your line will quickly begin to drift downstream. Mend to control drag as needed. Follow your fly and line downstream with your rod and throw stack mends if you need to put slack in your line to extend your drift on the water as your fly, leader and line pass your position (2). This will avoid drag from occurring and lengthen your presentation. Continue to follow your line with your rod toward your target and at the end of your presentation you can let you fly hang in the current as your line tightens at the end of the drift (3). If you are using a wet fly, the pause will raise the depth of the fly which can help to entice a strike. A reach cast may be helpful with this type of presentation because it can help you prevent drag.

ACROSS PRESENTATION

An across stream presentation increases the chance for drag to occur because you may be casting directly across multiple currents (fast and slow). A reach, Tug or Slack cast can help with this type of presentation.

MAKING AN ACROSS STREAM PRESENTATION

Enter the river cautiously to avoid frightening the fish with any debris that you may dislodge when you wade in the water (1). Cast across with a slack, parachute, or tuck/tug cast to put some slack quickly on the water (2). Mend if needed to eliminate drag but most likely the current will remove any slack in your line (3). Follow your fly and line downstream with your rod and throw stack mends to put slack on the water as your fly, leader and line pass your position (4). This will avoid drag from occurring and lengthen your presentation. Let you fly hang in the current at the end of your presentation and you can raise and lower your rod tip to animate your fly (5).

DOWN & ACROSS PRESENTATION

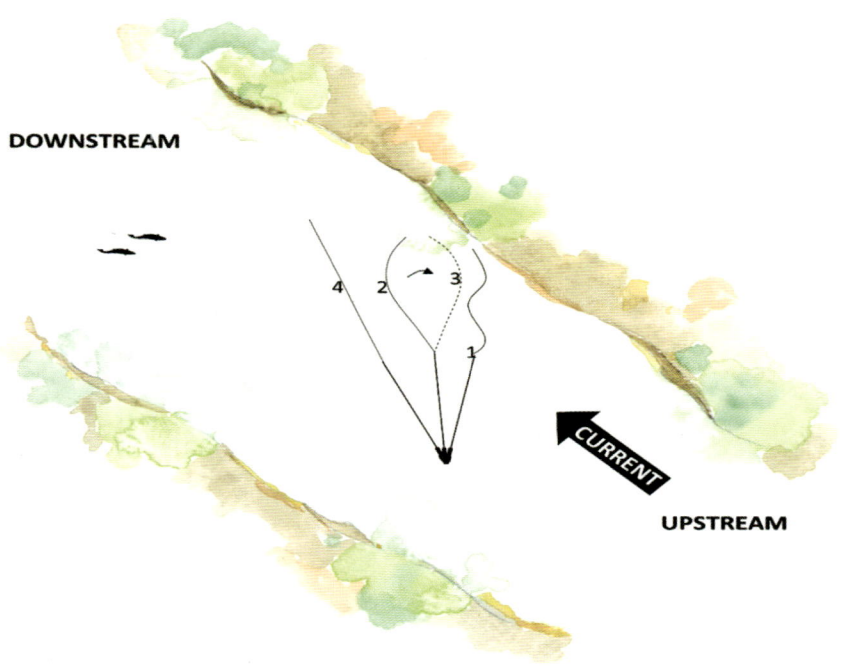

A downstream and across presentation means that your fly will reach the fish first before your leader or line. You will need to avoid drag by mending or suing a Tug or Slack cast. One advantage to this presentation is that you do not have to cast over fish and potentially frighten them.

READING THE WATER

MAKING A DOWNSTREAM AND ACROSS PRESENTATION

Enter the water upstream from your target and be very cautious not to kick up too much debris while wading because it will travel downstream and potentially frighten the fish. You often have to get out toward the middle of a river to make this presentation effectively. Cast downstream and across with a slack, parachute or tuck/tug cast so you put slack in your line at the start (1). Mend if needed (2 & 3). Follow your line with your rod as it drifts downstream and make stack mends to lengthen your presentation and avoid drag. Let you fly hang in the current as your line tightens at the end of the drift. If no strike occurs, mend toward the bank and strip in your line (4).

DOWNSTREAM PRESENTATION

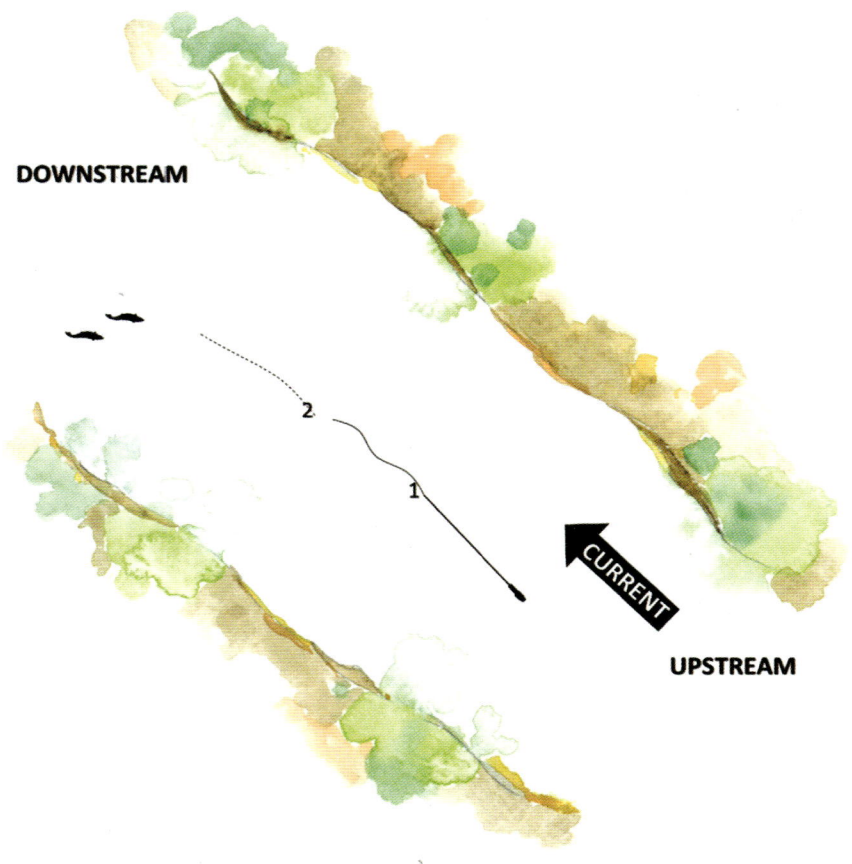

A downstream presentation is similar to the downstream and across cast. This means that your fly will reach the fish first before your leader or line. You will need to avoid drag by mending and add slack as needed so a Slack cast and stack mend will help you avoid drag.

READING THE WATER

MAKING A DOWNSTREAM PRESENTATION

Enter the water upstream from your target and be cautious not to kick up debris while wading because it will travel downstream and frighten the fish. Cast directly downstream with a slack, tuck/tug, or parachute cast to immediately put slack on the water. Throw stack mends to add slack into your presentation and avoid drag.

Follow your line with your rod as it drifts downstream and make stack mends to lengthen your presentation and avoid drag.

Let you fly hang in the current as your line

STRATEGIES
Technique and Tips

HIGH STICKING

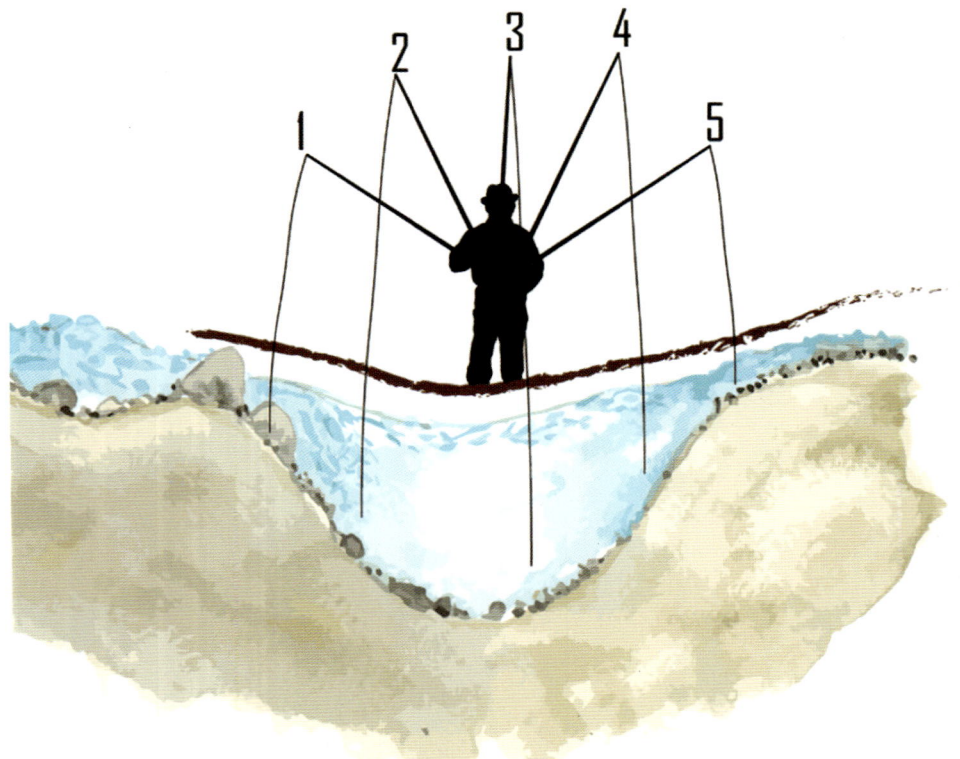

High sticking can be done with a dry or wet fly in close to your position in the water or from the edge of the bank of a river or stream. There is not a lot of opportunity for drag to occur because almost all of your line and the majority of your leader is kept off the surface of the water. This type of presentation is very similar to an induced fly strategy where you are trying to make your fly act like the insect you are trying to imitate to entice the fish to strike. This technique is often used with a nymph wet fly.

STRATEGIES

Steps:

Enter the water downstream from your target, if possible, to avoid frightening the fish with the debris that you will kick up while wading.

Lob or toss your fly upstream close to your position with your rod tip high keeping all of your line and the majority of your leader off the water (1). If you are using a strike indicator, that should float on the surface and the rest of your leader and line should be off the water.

Follow your fly downstream as it drifts keeping your rod tip high in the air to keep you line off the water (2 – 4).

Let your fly hang downstream in the current for a few seconds after it has drifted all the way downstream of your position. Animate your fly by moving your rod tip up and down (5). You can lower your rod tip and add line onto the water to extend your presentation downstream if you like at the end of your high stick.

HIGH STICKING

BANKING

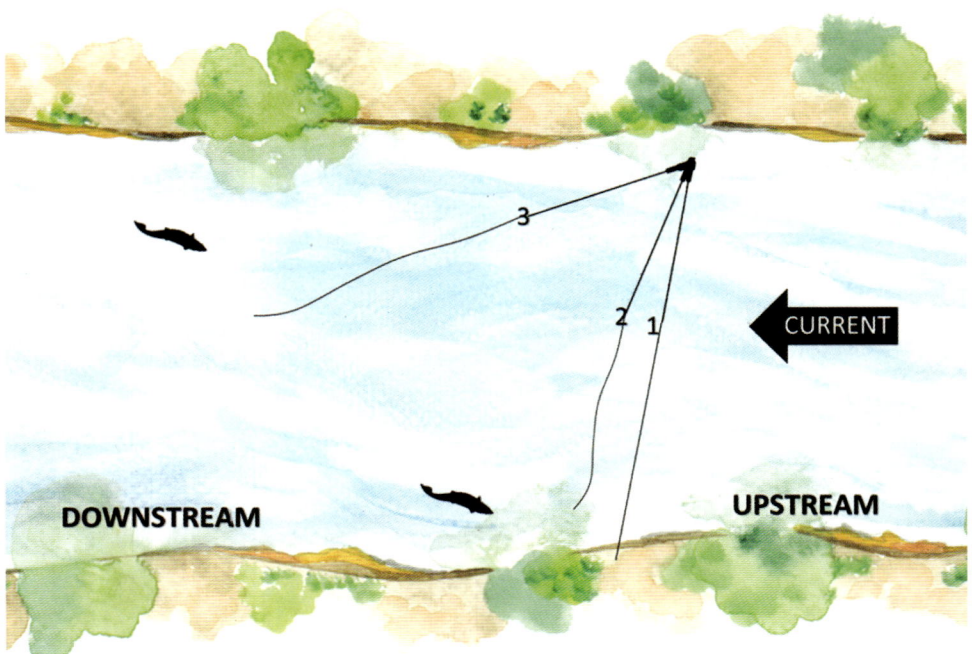

A bank presentation is useful for flies that imitate insects that might jump or fall off riverbanks, from tree branches that hang over the river, or may get blown off plants into the water. Flies that imitate grasshoppers, ants, spiders, frogs, mice, etc. are perfect to try with this strategy. This is also a good strategy to try with undercut banks.

1. Enter the water downstream from your target, if possible, to avoid frightening the fish with any debris that you' might kick up while wading. Cast your fly across and onto the bank or as close to the edge as possible to make the most natural presentation. Make sure not to cast into weeds or grass that will snag your fly.
2. Quickly pull your fly off the bank into the water before your line is taken downstream by the current and causes drag.
3. If no strike occurs, let your fly drift downstream. Throw stack mends to lengthen the drift. When you fly has drifted downstream, let the current remove the slack from your line and swing your fly toward the bank.

OTHER STRATEGIES

Soft Hackle

Soft hackle flies are simple patterns tied with floss or thread bodies and partridge hackle feathers tied in at the head that imitate everything from insect legs to emerging wings. They usually take longer to sink because they are tied sparsely.

One way to present a soft hackle fly is to cast across and slightly downstream far enough ahead of your target to give the fly time to sink to the desired depth. Swing your fly across the current and animate it by raising your rod tip and/or let the current tighten your line to imitate an emerging insect. You can also twitch the fly with some short strips of line to make the hackle feathers pulse. Allow your fly to hang in the current at the end of your presentation before stripping it in. You can also make this presentation upstream if you control your slack and drag.

Poppers

Poppers are buoyant dry flies that imitate insects, amphibians, etc. that swim on the surface of the current. Poppers are usually tied with deer hair packed together or tied with foam. You will not need to cast these flies gently because you usually want them to splash onto the water and make the same type of splash as the frog or mouse you are typing to imitate would do. Try casting the popper across and on or close to a bank as possible and quickly pull it off the bank into the water. This can work well on an overhung bank where fish may be hiding underneath. After you cast, let your fly dead drift downstream and you can animate your fly by stripping it in with small or large strips and twitches. If you think your fly might get caught in the bushes or weeds on the bank be careful. You don't want to lose a fly this way.

Terrestrials

Terrestrial flies can be fished alone or as a dual fly rig. Try a hopper as your lead fly and drift a beetle, other terrestrial pattern, or wet fly as the dropper. Two high floating patterns make for a very buoyant dual fly setup. Try attaching a wet fly to your terrestrial to cover two different depths at the same time. Fish terrestrials near semi-submerged objects in the water, near banks, under weeds that hang over a bank, or over weeds growing in the water.

Wet Flies

Depth and animation are important to consider when you are presenting a wet fly. Imitate the behavior of what fish are eating and use any of the presentations in the previous chapter. Casts like the tuck/tug help to make your fly sink quicker into the water.

Dry Flies

Depth and animation are not factors when fishing dry flies. Eliminating drag is critical and selecting the right dry fly based on what and how fish are eating in also important (are they eating insects floating on the surface of the water, emerging, etc.).

NYMPHS

Learning how to fish with nymphs is an important skill because approximately 80% or more of what fish eat live under the surface of the water and are mostly e available as food to fish all year long.

Nymphs are presented below the surface of the water usually near the bottom depending on what life cycle stage fish are feeding on at the time. Nymphs are tied with weight on the shank of the hook but additional weight may need to be added depending on the depth you are trying to achieve. Wet flies drifting below the surface make it difficult sometimes to detect strikes so you can use a strike indicator or watch the tip of your colored line to detect a strike (this is one reason fly lines are made so colorful).

You can add weight onto your leader if your nymph is not sinking fast enough to the depth of the water your desire. Weight should be placed 8-24 inches above the fly and just enough weight should be added so your nymph does not drag along the bottom (see image on page 139).

STRATEGIES

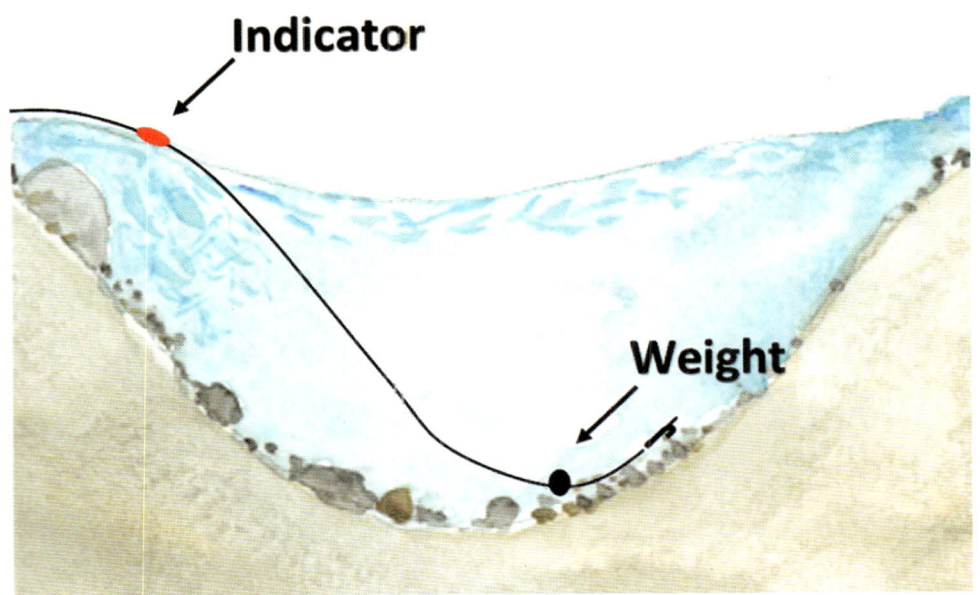

BASIC SWING STYLE OR DEAD DRIFT NYMPH PRESENTATION

Nymphs are presented close to your position where you are wading so it is important to be as stealthy as possible. You can also nymph while standing on the bank or on a rock or hiding behind a bush while putting your rod over the top over the water. Make a short cast close to your position (1) and only use enough line or leader to reach the depth you need. I usually keep the tip of my rod high and adjust the depth of my nymph by raising or lowering my rod tip. Follow the tip of your rod keeping the end of your line or strike indicator vertically aligned with your rod tip as it moves downstream (2). You can animate the fly if you raise or lower the tip of your rod to adjust its depth. Continue to follow your line with the tip of your rod and swing downstream (3). You can release line at the end of your presentation if you want to let your fly drift downstream. At the end of your presentation stop releasing line and your nymph will rise up toward the surface of the water imitating an emerging insect.

STREAMERS

Streamers represent a range of food like baitfish, leeches, minors, crustaceans, etc. They are also used as "searching" patterns of flies when you are not sure what food is available to fish.

You can animate streamers to imitate the behavior of what the fish are eating or to attract a fish to strike. Some basic streamer animations include: stripping in the line at different speeds and pausing in between strips, raising and lowering the rod tip, flicking the tip of your rod, retrieving your streamer in faster in shallow water to prevent it from dragging on the bottom of the river or stream, or switch colors and/or size.

PRESENTATION OF A STREAMER TO A POOL

Start upstream above the head of a pool and cast downstream ahead of the slowest part of the pool (1). Give you streamer enough slack (but not too much because the current at the head of the pool will start to slow down. Give your streamer enough time to sink to the depth you desire.

STRATEGIES

If nothing strikes at the head of the pool, let your streamer drift into the deepest part of the pool in the middle and continue to feed slack as needed to avoid drag (2). At the end of your presentation, you can strip in some line and raise the tip of your rod to adjust the depth of your streamer.

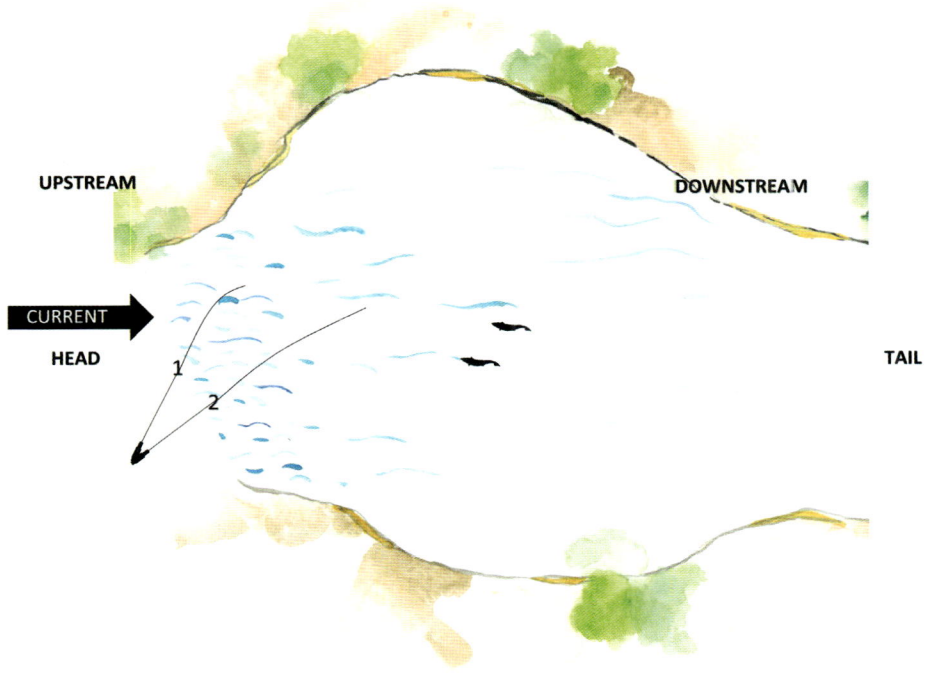

STREAMERS

MULTIPLE FLY

A multiple fly rig combines flies together on the same leader and enables you to offer fish different choices and/or drift flies at different depths of water at the same time.

The fly closest to you is known as the leader and the fly at the end is known as the dropper. The distance between your flies will vary depending on the types of flies you use and the depth where you want your flies to drift. Multiple fly rigs are heavier, so they are more difficult to cast. Avoid false casts, use shorter, slower casting strokes, and throw more open loop to avoid tangles. The illustration below shows you how far apart to separate your flies.

Multiple flies can be connected together in several ways:

BEND CONNECTION

Snip off a length of tippet that you will use to tie the dropper fly to the lead fly. The length of tippet is determined by the depth of the water and how deep or far apart you want the dropper from the lead fly. Tie an improved clinch knot to the bend of the lead fly and the eye of the dropper fly.

TWO EYE CONNECTION

Snip off a length of tippet, tie the lead fly to your leader, tie the extra tippet to the eye of the lead fly, and then tie the dropper fly to the end of the tippet.

TAG CONNECTION

Tie the lead fly to your leader but leave 16 - 36 inches of leader hanging and tie the dropper fly to the end of the extra hanging section of leader.

STRATEGIES

DROPPER LOOP CONNECTION

Tie a dropper loop in your leader, tie a piece of tippet to a second fly, and connect the tag end of the tippet to the loop in your leader. This type of connection helps keep your flies from getting tangled.

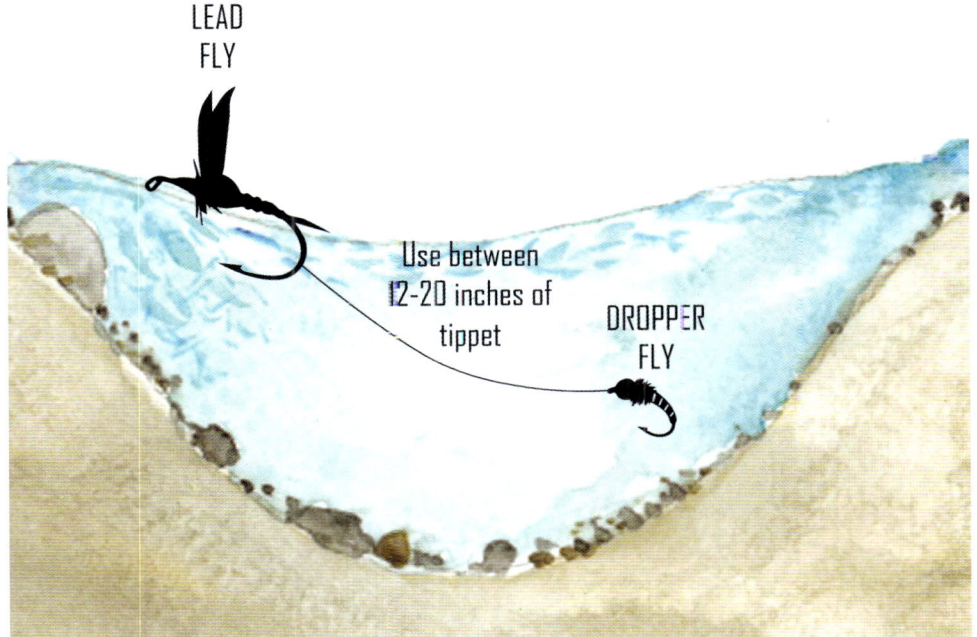

LEAD FLY

Use between 12-20 inches of tippet

DROPPER FLY

MULTIPLE FLY | 151

TYPES OF MULTIPLE FLY SETUPS:

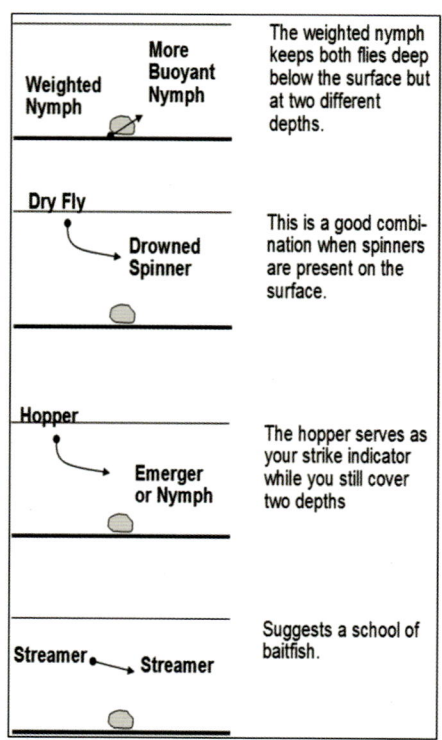

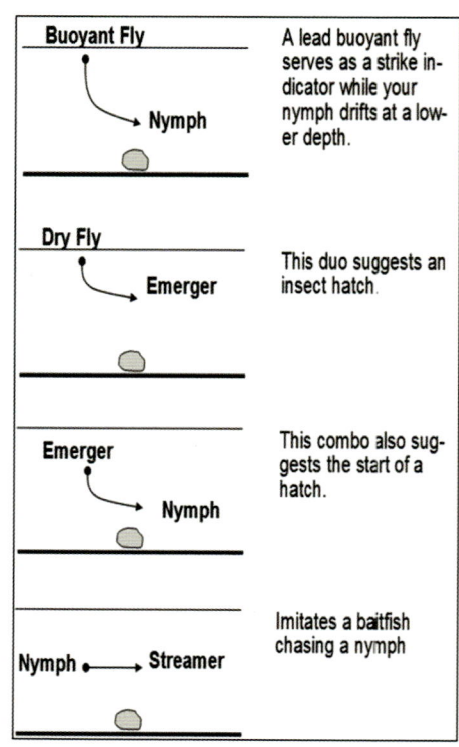

STRATEGIES

JOURNAL NOTES

Location: _____

Date/Time: _____

Equipment Used:

Weather Conditions:

Water Conditions:

Visible Rise Forms:

STRATEGIES

Insects Present:

Successful Presentation:

RELATED TITLES

Fishing the Canadian Rockies 2nd Edition is an updated, revised and comprehensive guidebook to the lakes, rivers and streams of the Canadian Rockies. The area covered by Fishing the Canadian Rockies, extends from the Canada-U.S. border in the south, through Jasper, Switzer and Mt. Robson parks in the north. Both the Alberta and British Columbia sides of the Continental Divide through the Rockies are covered.

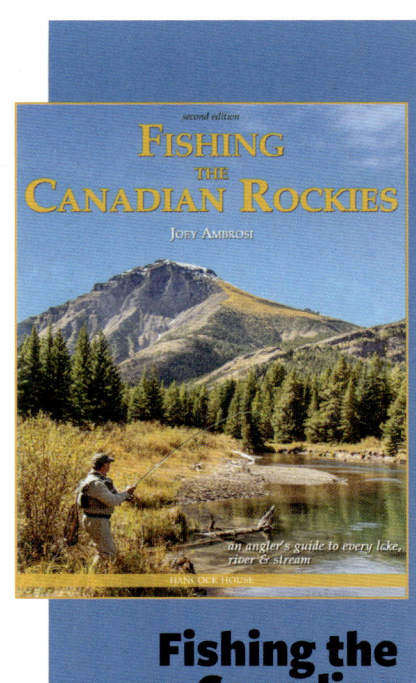

Fishing the Canadian Rockies

Ambrosi, Joey

978-0-88839-425-5 [paperback]
978-0-88839-349-4 [epub]
8½ x 11, sc, 248pp

$39.95

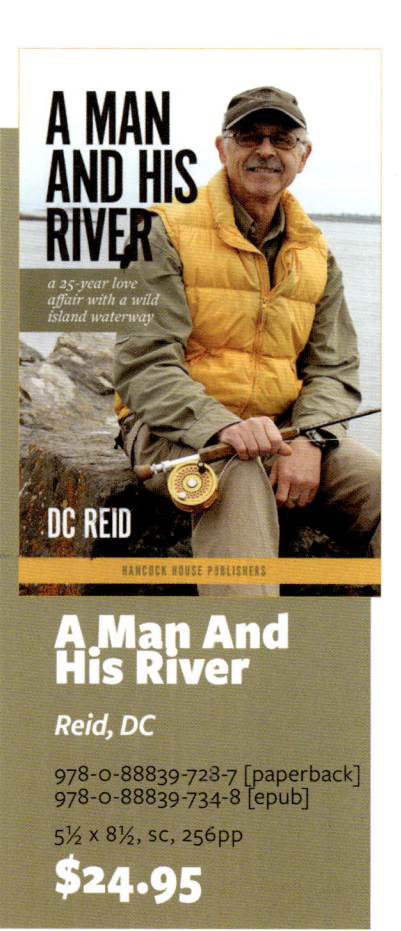

A Man And His River

Reid, DC

978-0-88839-723-7 [paperback]
978-0-88839-734-8 [epub]

5½ x 8½, sc, 256pp

$24.95

A 25-Year Love Affair with a Wild Island Waterway

A Man and His River is a love story, and a story of personal journey set on the banks of the Nitinat river on Vancouver Island. It is about the inherent and universal feeling of being near flowing water and the experiences of nature and wildlife that share the banks. This book is also a summary of the author's lifetime of fishing Vancouver Islands 123 watersheds and the pursuits of its diversity of salmon and trout.

Flying Tying: Proven flies from the Pacific Northwest

It is easy for the novice fly-fisher to become overwhelmed by the proliferation of items and gear that can be used to create artificial flies. Fly Tying- Proven Flies for the Pacific Northwest, provides a simple overview of the basic equipment, materials and patterns used for chironomids, wet flies, and dry flies as well as those for steelhead and salmon. Focusing on established flies that have years of proven success in the Pacific Northwest region, this book provides a combination of instruction as well as life lessons and stories accumulated over decades, providing both a useful and enjoyable read.

Fly Tying

Haaheim, Don

978-0-88839-768-3 [paperback]

5½ x 8½, sc, 208pp

$24.95

Black River Dreams: Meditations on fly fishing

Maximilian Werner

978-0-88839-633-4 [paperback]
5½ x 8½, sc, 172pp

$19.95

A celebration of fly fishing, alternately lyrical and meditative, mystical and sensuous, each of these 16 essays represents an exploration of the intersection between past and present, spirit and body, water and land, trout and people, ghosts and dreams. Whether Werner is describing his first and last time fly fishing as a boy on a stream in northern Maine or the golden evenings he and his wife cast to Apache trout cruising in the dim mountain light, he brings an ecologically informed, poetic sensibility to all of his fly-fishing encounters.

The Tactical Secrets of Lake Fishing

This straightforward fishing guide was written for the average fisherman. The focus is on tactics and a handful of secrets that keep fishing simple and enjoyable. These secrets are really a set of easy and logical processes that answer three basic questions: Where should I fish? What do I fish with? When do I fish? The key is in the relationship between trout and their changing ecology, and understanding how complex behavior is really a set of simple and predictable patterns. Ed looks at the basic physiology and instincts of fish and ends up with proven methods for catching fish. No other book so vividly related behavioral science to angling tactics.

ED RYCHKUN

TROUT FISHING

The Tactical Secrets of Lake Fishing

Trout Fishing

Rychkun, Ed

978-0-88839-338-8 [paperback]

5½ x 8½, sc, 120pp

$16.95

The 12 Basic Skills of Fly Fishing

Peck, Ted & Ed Rychkun

978-0-88839-392-0 [paperback]
5½ x 8½, sc, 42pp

$11.95

Authors Ted Peck and Ed Rychkun cut through the mystique and complexity surrounding fly fishing and come up with the twelve basic skills needed to understand and enjoy the engrossing art of fly fishing. Here they present a breakdown of fly fishing basics for the beginner. Covering topics such as the selection of equipment, holding a fly rod, mastering the roll cast, stripping the line, handling and landing fish- this book covers everything the beginner needs to know.